ALA Editions • **SPECIAL REPORTS**

OPEN ACCESS

WHAT YOU NEED TO KNOW NOW

WALT CRAWFORD

AMERICAN LIBRARY ASSOCIATION
Chicago   2011

Walt Crawford was a senior analyst at RLG for several decades, and more recently editorial director of the Library Leadership Network. He is now a semiretired writer and occasional speaker on libraries, technology, policy, and media. Since 2001 he has written and published the ejournal *Cites & Insights*. His published books include *First Have Something to Say: Writing for the Library Profession* (2003); *Being Analog: Creating Tomorrow's Libraries* (1999); *Future Libraries: Dreams, Madness and Reality* (with Michael Gorman, 1995); and eleven others going back to *MARC for Library Use: Understanding the USMARC Formats* (1984), along with several self-published books including *Balanced Libraries: Thoughts on Continuity and Change* (2007). Crawford has also published more than 500 articles and columns. In 1995, he received the American Library Association's LITA/Library Hi Tech Award for Excellence in Communication for Continuing Education, followed by the ALCTS/Blackwell Scholarship Award in 1997. He was president of the Library and Information Technology Association in 1992/93.

Printed in the United States of America

15   14   13   12   11   5   4   3   2   1

While extensive effort has gone into ensuring the reliability of the information in this book, the publisher makes no warranty, express or implied, with respect to the material contained herein.

Note that any URLs referenced in this volume, which were valid at the time of first print publication, may have changed prior to electronic publication.

ISBN: 978-0-8389-1106-8

Crawford, Walt.
   Open access : what you need to know now / by Walt Crawford.
      p. cm. — (ALA Editions special report)
   Includes bibliographical references and index.
   ISBN 978-0-8389-1106-8 (alk. paper)
   1. Open access publishing. I. Title.
   Z286.O63C73 2011
   070.5'7973 — dc22

                                                                        2011004933

Series cover design by Casey Bayer. Series text design in Palatino Linotype and Avenir by Karen Sheets de Gracia. Composition by Patricia Galarza-Hernandez.

♾ This paper meets the requirements of ANSI/NISO Z39.48-1992 (Permanence of Paper).

ALA Editions also publishes its books in a variety of electronic formats. For more information, visit the ALA Store at www.alastore.ala.org and select eEditions.

CONTENTS

ACKNOWLEDGMENTS

Thanks to all those who have written about open access, and always to my wife, Linda Driver, for encouraging my writing.

Special thanks to Dorothea Salo, Peter Suber, and Charles W. Bailey Jr., who reviewed the draft version of this book and offered valuable comments and criticisms. Failings in the final version are, of course, mine.

1

WHO
CARES?

Researchers and scholars give away the results of their work, most commonly in the form of peer-reviewed journal articles, so that others can benefit from that work and build on it (and so their work will be recognized and have impact). We gain the most as a society and as individuals when that's a symmetric process—when researchers and others can use those results without economic or other barriers.

That, in a nutshell, is what open access (OA) is all about. Open access literature is available online to be read for free by anyone, anytime, anywhere—as long as they have Internet access.

That's a simple definition that surrounds a complex set of issues and definitions. This Special Report lays out some of those issues, shows areas where librarians can become effective advocates for OA and guides you to other resources for understanding, tracking and using OA.

First consider the question above: Who cares? More specifically, why should *you* and your library care about OA?

THE SHORT VERSION

Academic librarians and special librarians should care about OA for several reasons, including these:

- OA means that researchers and practitioners among your patrons can take advantage of the latest work in their field of interest without adding to your library's resource burdens.
- Your library almost certainly cannot provide all the journal literature that might be useful to your patrons. OA gets past that limitation.
- Your library budget is being squeezed by online and print journal costs—particularly in the fields of science, technology, engineering, and medicine (STEM)—that grow much faster than inflation and leave little or no room for acquisitions in other areas. Widespread OA can ease that burden, allowing a more balanced set of expenditures in the future.

Public librarians should care about OA for more general reasons, including these:

- Effective open access speeds research and reduces wasted efforts by assuring that researchers can stay fully up to date on what's already been done. That benefits us all.
- You have practitioners and other patrons who need to know more about special topics in health and other areas where the journal literature is important, and still more patrons who wish to explore specialized areas. OA means your patrons can explore and learn as freely and as deeply as they choose.
- Chances are, there are independent researchers and scholars within your community—research and scholarship isn't limited to universities, colleges, and research labs. Those researchers and scholars need access to the journal literature just as much as institutional scholars. OA is the only plausible way to provide that access.

School librarians should care about OA for the same reasons *all* citizens should care about OA. Those reasons have to do with equity, access, fairness, and improved research productivity. They're explored in more detail in "The Moral and Pragmatic Case for Open Access," below.

I Heard About an Article that Concerns Me . . .

Consider a simple scenario. You or one of your patrons has read two newspaper articles describing research results you want to know more about. Maybe your patron has an obscure disease and the articles discuss promising research toward cures. Maybe you're tracking a new technology and the articles discuss important developments. One of the newspaper articles cites an article in *PLoS Biology* or *PLoS One*—or an article from any of a number of high energy–physics journals. The second cites an article in a journal that's either prestigious and very expensive or obscure and not readily available. (What does very expensive mean? Quite a few journals cost more than $10,000 per year for institutional subscriptions, and bundles of online journals can cost libraries hundreds of thousands or millions of dollars per year. Individual article charges can readily run $30 or more, when individual articles are even available.)

In the second case, you may not be able to read the journal article itself—a vitally important step, especially given the mixed quality of science and medical writing in most newspapers and online sources. If you or your patron can, it will be because your library is spending substantial sums of money to support that access, because somebody pays a significant sum for a copy of the particular article, or because you're (eventually) able to acquire an ILL copy within the tight restrictions on article lending and borrowing. For an obscure journal, even finding ways to acquire the article may cause delays.

In the first case, neither delays nor cost are involved. As long as you or your patron has access to the Internet (and nearly all public libraries provide such access), the journal article is freely and immediately available to read and save for further use.

That's OA in action: making research more useful and readers better informed.

THE MORAL AND PRAGMATIC CASE FOR OPEN ACCESS

Here's how John Willinsky puts it in *The Access Principle*: "A commitment to the value and quality of research carries with it a responsibility to extend the circulation of this work as far as possible, and ideally to all who are interested in it and might profit by it."[1]

Given the current state of technology, "as far as possible" appears to be open access. That doesn't reach the ideal, as only about 25 percent of the world's population has Internet access in 2010, but it's a huge improvement over known alternatives. Articles available through some version of OA are immediately available to anybody who's interested and might benefit, as long as they have Internet access—with no delay and no price or permission barriers.

That's a phenomenal change, a situation nearly unimaginable a few decades ago and nowhere near universality now. Peter Suber calls this the last-mile problem for knowledge, comparable to the last-mile problem faced by telecommunications providers (that is, getting the signal that last mile to each individual house or business):

> We're facing a last-mile problem for knowledge. We're pretty good at doing research, writing it up, vetting it, publishing it, and getting it to locations (physical libraries and web sites) close to users. We could be better at all those things, but any problems we encounter along the way are early- or mid-course problems. The last-mile problem is the one at the end of the process: making individualized connections to all the individual users who need to read that research.
>
> The last-mile problem for knowledge is not new. Indeed, for all of human history until recently it has been inseparable from knowledge itself and all our technologies for sharing it. It's only of interest today because the internet and OA give us unprecedented means for solving it, or at least for closing the gap significantly.[2]

The breakdown of OA arguments into moral and pragmatic issues that follows is Peter Suber's. (Some of these points are paraphrased and expanded from a list in Peter Suber's "Open access and the self-correction of knowledge.")[3]

Moral Arguments for Open Access

First and foremost, OA reduces access barriers for readers and authors alike. Discovery may still be an issue, but again—if you can get to the Internet and if the article's OA (and if you understand the language or trust Internet translation tools), you can read it.

The Budapest Open Access Initiative—the document that, more than any other, established *open access* as a term—includes this straightforward argument: "Removing access barriers to this literature will accelerate research, enrich education, share the learning of the rich with the poor and the poor with the rich, make this literature as useful as it can be, and lay the foundation for uniting humanity in a common intellectual conversation and quest for knowledge."

Libraries serve as the intellectual commons for many communities. Open access expands that commons by returning the results of research and scholarship to the commons. It also serves the community by eliminating wealth as a precursor for access.

Open access specifically serves the underserved, those least able to acquire scholarship either through library support or through direct contact with the authors. Open access also substitutes an abundance of access for the artificial scarcity created through traditional subscription mechanisms—and serves to counter inappropriate distribution of knowledge by making it universally available.

Scholars and researchers write journal articles for impact and communication rather than to make money. Open access fulfills this motivation by making those articles as widely available as is currently possible—and, in so doing, returns the control of scholarship to the scholars themselves.

Finally, for that very large subset of research supported by public funds (e.g., the many billions of dollars of NIH-funded research), open access is an issue of fundamental fairness to the taxpayers, those who paid for the research in the first place.

Pragmatic Arguments for Open Access

By making all existing research available to anyone wishing to use it, OA accelerates the research process and makes researchers and practitioners more productive. It also makes research more useful by making outcomes directly available to a wider audience, thus increasing the research funder's return on investment. In other words, OA is simply good business for the research community.

Open access also helps authors find readers—and readers find authors. It means that articles can reach a wider audience at a lower cost than is feasible through subscriptions and licensing. Open access unquestionably saves money for readers. It should also save money for researchers and for libraries.

Journals benefit from OA because published articles are more discoverable and useful. Gold OA journals can attract more readers, authors, and related funding sources. Traditional journals supporting full green OA (with fully edited articles deposited immediately into repositories) gain similar benefits. Agencies funding research also benefit from OA because the results of their funding can reach much wider audiences and be used more effectively in future research and practice.

Enlarging the intellectual commons sounds nice and is an excellent moral argument. The pragmatic equivalent is that open access builds stronger communities of researchers and users alike, widens dialogue within and among these communities, and can support better cooperation within and among the communities.

Libraries are also about long-term access. Open access can improve preservation prospects by making it feasible to copy articles and sets of articles and to migrate materials to new platforms as needed.

Some varieties of open access aren't just about reading. To the extent that OA becomes full open access, it can help create new knowledge by allowing text mining, data crunching, automated summarizing, and other computer-assisted techniques.

Finally, open access improves the reliability of inquiry. It invites the whole world to find faults with claims made by scientists and scholars. As Peter Suber says:

> OA facilitates the testing and validation of knowledge claims. OA en-
> hances the process by which science is self-correcting. OA improves

the reliability of inquiry. . . . [W]e must issue "a standing invitation to the whole world" to find fault with our knowledge claims. This requires disseminating our claims as widely as possible. We don't have to compel everyone to read our work and comment on it. . . . But we do have to make our claims available to everyone who might care to read and comment on them.[4]

THE SPECIAL CASE OF ACADEMIC AND SPECIAL LIBRARIES

The case for open access applies to all libraries and librarians, and should be strong enough to convince forward-thinking librarians to support OA and help move it forward. For academic libraries and many special libraries (specifically those that support researchers), there's another set of arguments, having to do with the roles of libraries and financial realities.[5]

Libraries need to provide both strong physical collections and access to resources beyond those physical collections. Academic libraries should do their best to assure long-term access to resources in all disciplines, including those disciplines where the primary publication method is the monograph. Libraries should acquire, organize, and secure long-term access to the things that make us a civilization, the thinking, knowledge and wisdom set down in articles, books, and other media.

Effective long-term access involves several interrelated issues, including:

- The money to acquire physical resources and provide access to other resources, and to pay the professional staff to determine what to acquire
- The means—money and procedures—to assure effective access, through cataloging and other organization and discovery techniques
- The wherewithal—determination, money, and procedures—to preserve physical works and digital resources and assure that future generations can use those resources

Science, technology, engineering, and medicine (STEM) consume most of the serial budgets of most academic libraries. Indeed, STEM journals consume most of the total acquisitions and access budgets of most academic libraries. But refereed STEM journal articles aren't all there is to science, technology, engineering, and medicine, and certainly not all there is to scholarly and human creativity.

Even in STEM, monographs play a role, as do working papers, datasets, and other "gray" materials that don't fit into the refereed-journal-article mold. Outside—in the humanities and social sciences—monographs and other books may be the primary means of communicating progress. For that matter, serial publications other than refereed scholarly journals play significant roles in the record of human creativity that should be the stuff of libraries.

The Current Journal Model Is Broken and Getting Worse

Too many STEM journals cost too much money, and increase in price at too rapid a rate, for libraries to sustain the level of access they need. The cost of STEM journal access distorts library budgets, driving out the less expensive journals and monographs and other resources. The current model, with several large commercial publishers dominating the field of STEM publishing and charging what they believe the market will bear, is unsustainable. It is already breaking down, with even the wealthiest libraries canceling large numbers of journals.

It's also getting worse because more research leads to even more specialized, journals, most of them from commercial publishers—and if researchers need those journals, that places even more pressure on existing resources. For example (as reported at *Ars Technica* in an item most recently updated on August 18, 2010), one recent study found that 23 new journals for stem cell research have been established since 2004—going from three journals entirely focused on stem cells in 2004 to 18 at this point, and from eight with relevant overlaps to stem cell research to 16.

It is apparent that some major commercial publishers fully intend to charge what the market will bear. They have succeeded in acquiring most of the highest-profile journals, including many that were originally modestly priced society-published journals, and in raising prices so as to assure profit margins far in excess of those enjoyed by most book publishers and companies in other industries.

I am not arguing that these publishers don't add value. Clearly they do. I am arguing that the subscription model simply will not stand: it is already breaking down and will continue to break down, probably at an accelerating rate.

The current model is also broken from a philosophical perspective: it makes it more difficult for scholars, researchers, and practitioners, especially independents and those at smaller institutions, to keep up with work in their field.

Open access strives to correct the philosophical breakage. When OA becomes nearly complete, and to the extent that OA is provided through OA journals (see chapter 2), it can also help correct the financial breakage.

Open access journals can relieve cost pressures on libraries. Open access journals can reduce the cost structure of the entire scholarly publishing enterprise. Libraries may even be sensible candidates to carry out the organizational tasks involved in publishing an electronic-only open access journal.

The current journal model didn't just start breaking down recently. For example, the University of California, Berkeley carried out significant serial budget cuts more than thirty years ago because its budget couldn't keep up with price increases. (I know; I was there.) But it's getting worse . . . enough worse that, despite the best efforts of commercial publishers to assure us that everything's OK, it's clear that things must change.

The University of California and the Nature Publishing Group

Here's just one example of how bad things are getting, one that created a sensation. It's also an interesting example of how commercial publishers try to pit scholars against scholars and universities against universities. On June 4, 2010, the California Digital Library (CDL, which negotiates University of California–wide access arrangements) sent a letter to UC faculty members noting that Nature Publishing Group (NPG) proposed to quadruple UC's site license fees for 2011. CDL, on UC's behalf, pushed back—suggesting that CDL might have to suspend subscriptions to the 67 journals (including *Nature* itself) that UC currently buys access to, and that it might be time for a systemwide boycott of NPG journals, a voluntary boycott encouraging UC researchers not to contribute papers to NPG journals, review manuscripts for those journals, or serve on their editorial boards.

This is strong stuff—and, along with the letter, CDL noted some of the numbers about UC systemwide online journal subscriptions. About 8,000 journals are involved—at average costs for the ten-campus licenses between $3,000 and $7,000 per journal. The proposed NPG fee would raise the price per journal from a current $4,465 to more than $17,000. Meanwhile, UC faculty have contributed more than 5,000 articles to NPG journals over the past six years.

It's hard to believe that NPG thought a California public institution has additional funds in 2010 or didn't know CDL has been negotiating workable compromises with other publishers. But NPG, which increased the price of institutional print subscriptions for *Scientific American* from $50 to $300 after acquiring the magazine, apparently felt it could get away with it. A June 9, 2010, NPG press release accused CDL of "sensationalist use of data out of context" and "misrepresentation of NPG pricing policies" and seemed to suggest that other universities were actually subsidizing UC's access to NPG publications. More dueling press releases followed, with UC noting that NPG's average annual price increases were three times the rate of inflation and roughly as much per year as UC's materials budget increases over five years. If you want to dig deeper into the UC-NPG situation, recognizing that it's only one case out of many (but higher profile than most), you should have no trouble finding dozens of commentaries and source documents. One excellent commentary, noting the ancillary damage to humanities, came from Bethany Nowviskie on June 9, 2010, under the title "fight club soap"; I suggest reading it directly at http://nowviskie.org/2010/fight -club-soap/. Peter Suber discusses "California against Nature" in the July 2, 2010, *SPARC Open Access Newsletter* (www.earlham.edu/~peters/fos/newsletter/07-02-10 .htm), including not only several dozen links to elements of and commentaries on this particular conflict but also other items that put it in some context. This specific incident may not lead to immediate change—by late August 2010, a joint statement took a conciliatory tone and CDL was once again negotiating with NPG—but it's indicative. And it's not alone. Several other major institutions have either canceled bundles of journals or have plans to do so. This incident, although extreme, may be typical of what we're seeing and will continue to see as the existing subscription journal system breaks down. We have a respected publisher accusing a respected university of misrepresentation and misinformation, attempting to turn libraries and universities against one another, and seemingly suggesting that NPG was a more worthy recipient of a few last drops of blood from UC's budgetary turnip than other publishers. This behavior only makes sense in a time when the whole enterprise is beginning to crumble.

There's another issue here. The University of California includes an exceptionally large number of highly regarded researchers. It has real power when negotiating with publishers. Most universities, most colleges have nowhere near the negotiating power. If UC can't afford the journals its researchers need, even with substantial discounts, how can smaller institutions even hope to provide adequate access? Open access may be the only long-term answer to that question.

The Breaking Model Damages Secondary Players First

There's reason to believe that it isn't the big commercial publishers and their overpriced journals that will be hit first as the subscription model continues to crumble. The first to go tend to be journals with smaller audiences and lesser reputations, including many of the more reasonably priced journals and those in the humanities.

The breaking model causes one specific economic dislocation and clarifies another economic distortion. The economic dislocation: journal subscriptions shove out monograph and other acquisitions. Some libraries have protected monographic budgets, and that may be a partial solution. The economic distortion is more sensitive: libraries have been underwriting professional societies indirectly, and can no longer afford to do so.

In essence, academic libraries need open access if they're to continue any real semblance of maintaining long-term access to the records of the civilization. Harvard can't subscribe to everything that would serve its researchers—and neither can any other institution. From the smallest academic libraries to the largest, and including most special libraries, support for open access is important to the libraries' own long-term health and effectiveness.

A FEW WORDS ABOUT SCHOLARLY JOURNAL PUBLISHING

Before exploring open access further, you should understand the basics of scholarly journal publishing. Oversimplifying somewhat, here are the steps:

1. One or more scholars and researchers write an article describing the results of their research and scholarship. At this point, the authors automatically gain copyright in the article and can legally post the draft article.
2. The authors submit the article to a journal, where the article is reviewed by other scholars (peer review) and either accepted, rejected, or returned for revision. Almost all peer review is performed for free as part of scholarship, with the editor(s) managing the review process.
3. At some point between submission and acceptance, the publisher will require some written agreement from the authors—either assigning copyright to the publisher or granting specific right to the publisher. The consideration for this grant or assignment is not payment; it is publication. (Scholarly journal articles almost never involve payments *to* the authors, although the publisher may require payment *from* the authors or other agencies.)
4. The publisher carries out various tasks, including line editing, copy editing, proofreading, layout and markup, actual publication (print or electronic), and marketing or publicity. All of those tasks involve money or voluntary effort.

At the beginning of the process, the authors have clear legal rights to make the draft articles openly available, rights that may or may not continue past submission and acceptance. At the end of the process, access to either the submitted article or the published article—or some in-between state—depends on the agreements between the authors and publisher and the publisher's policies. The heart of open access is improving those agreements and policies to assure that articles are freely available once they're published.

CONCLUSION

Open access (OA) has enormous potential benefits for society as a whole and for your library and patrons in particular. That said, there's a lot more to consider—and you should be aware that this book is a quick overview of a field about which millions of words have been written.

Chapter 2, "Understanding the Basics," defines key terms in OA in more detail, cites some key documents and players, offers some notes on the state of OA in mid-2010, and considers predecessors to OA.

Chapter 3, "Issues for Open Access," considers some real issues involved in moving OA forward.

Chapter 4, "Open Access Controversies," considers two very different areas: a set of false controversies that opponents of OA continue to raise—and a different set of legitimate controversies.

Chapter 5, "Taking Action," suggests roles for libraries and librarians to be actively involved in the progress of OA.

Chapter 6, "Exploring Open Access," offers some resources for further investigation, including periodicals, blogs, books and others. Most (but not all) of these resources are themselves OA.

NOTES

1. John Willinsky, *The Access Principle* (Cambridge & London: The MIT Press, 2006).
2. Peter Suber, "Open access and the last-mile problem for knowledge," *SPARC Open Access Newsletter* #123 (July 2, 2008).
3. Peter Suber, "Open access and the self-correction of knowledge," *SPARC Open Access Newsletter* #122 (June 2, 2008).
4. Ibid.
5. Portions of this section originally appeared in different form in my essay "Thinking About Libraries and Access," which appeared in the June 2006 *Cites & Insights* (http://citesandinsights.info/civ6i8.pdf).

2
UNDERSTANDING THE
BASICS

Free online access to journal articles. What more do you need to know?

Quite a lot, as it happens—even if you agree with that six-word definition of open access. There's a reason this book begins with a longer definition, "Open access literature is available online to be read for free by anyone, anytime, anywhere—as long as they have Internet access." That definition expands OA to include more than just journal articles but also narrows the scope by saying "to be read." As you'll see in this chapter, that defines one flavor of OA, but it's not the flavor most desired by some researchers and advocates.

This chapter provides expanded definitions and key terms, considers the colors and flavors of open access, notes some of the terms that were used before *open access* emerged as a term, distinguishes some other "opens" that may or may not be related to OA, and considers the state of the field in mid-2010.

Consider a narrower and more stringent definition of open access:

> Open access requires that refereed journal articles be fully and freely available on the open Internet, on or before the date of formal publication, to be read, downloaded, distributed, printed, and used for any legal purpose (including text manipulation, datamining and other derivative purposes), without permission or other barriers.

See the differences? This definition restricts the universe to refereed journal articles, omitting many other kinds of content that appear in some journals. It explicitly provides for immediate access, not delayed access. Finally, it calls for much more than free reading—it calls for a range of other uses.

At this point, I believe most (but not all) open access advocates would regard all three definitions—the first sentence of this chapter, the definition from chapter 1, and the sentence set-off above—as correct, with the set-off version the most desirable. That hasn't always been the case and may not be the case in the future.

BUDAPEST, BETHESDA AND BERLIN

Three international meetings in 2002 and 2003 yielded statements that established *open access* as the common term for initiatives to make scholarly literature more widely and freely available. These statements were not the start of the movement for better access to the scholarly literature, but they're key defining points for the movement and the name *open access*.

Budapest Open Access Initiative

According to the website www.soros.org/openaccess, the Budapest Open Access Initiative (BOAI) "arises from a small but lively meeting convened in Budapest by the Open Society Institute (OSI) on December 1-2, 2001." The resulting statement appeared on February 14, 2002. Initially signed by 16 individuals, it has to date been endorsed by 5,278 individuals and 539 organizations from many nations.

Given the primacy of BOAI, it's worth quoting almost half of the 1,100-word document, omitting some argumentation at the beginning and in the middle (and a key moral argument already given in chapter 1):

> An old tradition and a new technology have converged to make possible an unprecedented public good. The old tradition is the willingness of scientists and scholars to publish the fruits of their research in scholarly journals without payment, for the sake of inquiry and knowledge. The new technology is the Internet. The public good they make possible is the world-wide electronic distribution of the peer-reviewed journal literature and completely free and unrestricted access to it by all scientists, scholars, teachers, students, and other curious minds. . . .
>
> For various reasons, this kind of free and unrestricted online availability, which we will call *open access*, has so far been limited to small portions of the journal literature. . . . [W]e call on all interested institutions and individuals to help open up access to the rest of this literature and remove the barriers, especially the price barriers, that stand in the way. . . .
>
> The literature that should be freely accessible online is that which scholars give to the world without expectation of payment. Primarily, this category encompasses their peer-reviewed journal articles, but it also includes any unreviewed preprints that they might wish to put online for comment or to alert colleagues to important research findings. . . .
> By "open access" to this literature, we mean its free availability on the public internet, permitting any users to read, download, copy, distribute, print, search, or link to the full texts of these articles, crawl them for indexing, pass them as data to software, or use them for any other lawful purpose, without financial, legal, or technical barriers other than those inseparable from gaining access to the Internet itself. The only constraint on reproduction and distribution, and the only role for copyright in this domain, should be to give authors control over the integrity of their work and the right to be properly acknowledged and cited.

. . . To achieve open access to scholarly journal literature, we recommend two complementary strategies.

1. Self-Archiving: First, scholars need the tools and assistance to deposit their refereed journal articles in open electronic archives, a practice commonly called self-archiving. When these archives conform to standards created by the Open Archives Initiative, then search engines and other tools can treat the separate archives as one. . . .
2. Open-access Journals: Second, scholars need the means to launch a new generation of journals committed to open access, and to help existing journals that elect to make the transition to open access. Because journal articles should be disseminated as widely as possible, these new journals will no longer invoke copyright to restrict access to and use of the material they publish. Instead they will use copyright and other tools to ensure permanent open access to all the articles they publish . . .

Open access to peer-reviewed journal literature is the goal. Self-archiving (1.) and a new generation of open-access journals (2.) are the ways to attain this goal. They are not only direct and effective means to this end, they are within the reach of scholars themselves, immediately, and need not wait on changes brought about by markets or legislation. . . .

Consider that boldfaced definition. It calls for virtually unlimited usage. Note also that this statement does not mark either OA strategy as the preferred or initial strategy.

George Soros' Open Society Institute provided funding for a range of OA-related initiatives following this statement including the *Directory of Open Access Journals* or *DOAJ* (discussed further in chapter 6).

Bethesda Statement on Open Access Publishing

This statement, released June 20, 2003, originated in a one-day meeting with two dozen participants held April 11, 2003, at the Howard Hughes Medical Institute. You'll find the full 1,800-word statement (including a meeting summary) at www.earlham .edu/~peters/fos/bethesda.htm. The document includes some interesting statements such as an affirmation of the principle "that only the intrinsic merit of the work, and not the title of the journal in which a candidate's work is published, will be considered in appointments, promotions, merit awards or grants." Here's how the Bethesda group defined "open access publication":

Definition of Open Access Publication

An Open Access Publication [1] is one that meets the following two conditions:

1. The author(s) and copyright holder(s) grant(s) to all users a **free, ir-revocable, worldwide, perpetual right of access to, and a license to copy, use, distribute, transmit and display the work publicly and to make and distribute derivative works, in any digital medium for any responsible purpose, subject to proper attribution of author-ship** [2], as well as the right to make small numbers of printed copies for their personal use.

2. A complete version of the work and all supplemental materials, including a copy of the permission as stated above, in a suitable standard electronic format **is deposited immediately upon initial publication in at least one online repository** that is supported by an academic institution, scholarly society, government agency, or other well-established organization that seeks to enable open access, un-restricted distribution, interoperability, and long-term archiving (for the biomedical sciences, PubMed Central is such a repository).

Notes:
1. Open access is a property of individual works, not necessarily jour-nals or publishers.
2. Community standards, rather than copyright law, will continue to provide the mechanism for enforcement of proper attribution and responsible use of the published work, as they do now.

Note three things here: the definition calls for essentially unlimited derivative use; it is in no way limited to journal articles or science, technology, and medicine; and deposit in a repository is a requirement for a publication to be considered OA.

Berlin Declaration on Open Access to Knowledge in the Sciences and Humanities

This document, "Berlin Declaration" for short, grew out of an October 20–22, 2003, conference in Berlin, held under the auspices of the Max Planck Society. You'll find the declaration and related notes, including a list of more than 200 organizations who have signed the declaration over the years, at http://oa.mpg.de/openaccess-berlin/berlindeclaration.html. The declaration explicitly notes the Budapest and Bethesda statements. Here are the goals and the first paragraph of the definition. The definition itself is nearly identical to the Bethesda definition, except that for the repository requirement, the phrase "in at least one online repository using suitable technical standards (such as the Open Archive definitions)" has been added after "one online repository," that deposit is considered publication, and the phrase "immediately upon publication" does not appear.

Goals

Our mission of disseminating knowledge is only half complete if the information is not made widely and readily available to society. New possibilities of knowledge dissemination not only through the classical form but also and increasingly through the open access paradigm via the Internet have to be supported. We define open access as a comprehensive source of human knowledge and cultural heritage that has been approved by the scientific community.

In order to realize the vision of a global and accessible representation of knowledge, the future Web has to be sustainable, interactive, and transparent. Content and software tools must be openly accessible and compatible.

Definition of an Open Access Contribution

Establishing open access as a worthwhile procedure ideally requires the active commitment of each and every individual producer of scientific knowledge and holder of cultural heritage. Open access contributions include original scientific research results, raw data and metadata, source materials, digital representations of pictorial and graphical materials, and scholarly multimedia material. (Actual definition follows, nearly identical to Bethesda.)

As of October 2003, then, there are three definitions for OA that all require full "responsible" derivative use and distribution, not only reading—and two of three that rely entirely on repositories, with no mention in the definitions of open access publishing itself (except for the assertion in the Berlin document that deposit in a repository constitutes publication).

Things have changed since then, largely to allow a broader range of actions to be called open access, even though they don't fully comply with these three statements (which Peter Suber calls the BBB statements).

COLORS AND FLAVORS

You'll see two colors commonly mentioned in discussions of OA and two other terms I'm calling "flavors": *green, gold, gratis,* and *libre*. Green and gold OA deal directly with two different approaches to providing free access to peer-reviewed scholarly journal articles, with little or no relevance to other material that might be made freely available. Gratis and libre, two flavors of open access, are relevant to all freely available material, including but not limited to peer-reviewed journal articles. In brief:

- Green OA consists of peer-reviewed articles deposited in freely accessible digital repositories (either subject or institutional).
- Gold OA consists of journals that make all peer-reviewed articles freely available for online reading at and after publication, with no fee or registration to read those articles.
- Gratis OA consists of articles (and other digital resources) that are readable for free online, but possibly no more than that.
- Libre OA consists of articles (and other digital resources) that have at least some additional forms of free usability beyond simple readability, ideally including all of those included in the Three B statements.

Let's look at each of those terms in more detail.

Green OA

Green open access—sometimes called "the green road to OA"—means depositing peer-reviewed articles at least as soon as they're published in freely accessible digital repositories (subject, institutional or otherwise). Most such repositories use the Open Archives Initiative Protocols for Metadata Harvesting (OAI-PMH), which help assure effective harvesting—but OAI-PMH is not a requirement for green OA. Articles must be complete full text (it's not enough to deposit abstracts). Articles may be in the form submitted to or approved by peer reviewers, sometimes called *preprint*, rather than the final post-review form, sometimes called *postprint*.

Green OA works best with OA archives or repositories. Here's what Peter Suber says about OA repositories in "A Very Brief Introduction to Open Access" (www.earlham .edu/~peters/fos/brief.htm):

> OA archives or repositories do not perform peer review, but simply make their contents freely available to the world. They may contain un-refereed preprints, refereed postprints, or both. Archives may belong to institutions, such as universities and laboratories, or disciplines, such as physics and economics. Authors may archive their preprints without anyone else's permission, and a majority of journals already permit authors to archive their postprints. When archives comply with the meta-data harvesting protocol of the Open Archives Initiative, then they are interoperable and users can find their contents without knowing which archives exist, where they are located, or what they contain. There is now open-source software for building and maintaining OAI-compliant archives and worldwide momentum for using it.

An earlier version of this statement included an additional sentence: "The costs of an archive are negligible: some server space and a fraction of the time of a technician." Peter Suber removed the sentence because most effective institutional repositories do much more than simply accept faculty preprints and postprints and can involve substantial expenses.

Sharp-eyed readers may notice another issue in the statement's penultimate sentence: "users can find their contents . . ."—which is true only if a search engine is harvesting the metadata and making it searchable in a free and useful manner.

OA repositories need not be limited to journal articles. *Institutional* repositories, specifically those within academic institutions, commonly serve as homes for a broader range of scholarly material—working papers, data sets, and the like. As long as metadata properly labels peer-reviewed articles as such, including the journal in which they appeared, there should be no confusion about the inclusion of non-peer-reviewed material within the same repository. For that matter, subject repositories need not be limited to peer-reviewed articles. It may be worth noting that many "green OA" journal articles at present aren't in repositories at all—they're on authors' personal websites.

There's a curious ambiguity about preprint deposits. As defined by some OA experts, these versions are the versions submitted to journals—prior to peer review. Given that peer review can lead to substantive as well as editorial changes in articles, a preprint might better be thought of as a draft. I've always thought of preprint deposits in terms of papers that have been accepted through peer review, but haven't yet been copy-edited and, in some cases, laid out for publication.

At one point, leading green OA advocate Stevan Harnad recommended that scholars deposit preprints along with correction sheets to allow readers to create the equivalent of the final paper and asserted that such deposits were always legitimate, regardless of the publisher's policies regarding open access. The first clause of the fourth sentence in the quoted paragraph above—"Authors may archive their preprints without anyone else's permission"—makes this assumption. The idea is that an author's transfer of copyright to a publisher only affects the published version. To the best of my knowledge, this assumption has not been tested in the courts. It is at least conceivable that a publisher could consider provision of free access to a marginally different text to be infringement, and it is certainly the case that a publisher's terms of publication could require, as a contractual matter, that no "preprint" version be available on an open archive. It's hard to say whether that's a real-world concern—whether any journal publisher would be willing to go that far in order to prevent access to draft articles. It's not out of the question, however. As recounted by Kevin Smith in a September 7, 2010, post at *Scholarly Communications @ Duke* (http://library.duke.edu/blogs/scholcomm), Knopf, the publisher of Raymond Carver's short stories, has threatened Carver's widow with a copyright infringement suit for her plans to publish the *original* versions of the stories—apparently heavily edited by Carver's editor at Knopf. That involves fiction for which Carver was paid, not scholarly articles for which authors are *not* paid, but those distinctions might not matter.

It's been suggested that OA archives or repositories "can provide OA by default to all their contents or can let authors control the degree of accessibility to their works."[1] That's true but unless authors provide immediate access to articles, those articles are not OA—even if they're in an OA repository. The repository at that point is a hybrid: part open, part closed. A hybrid repository makes sense for drafts, institutional records, working notes and other items, but if articles themselves have controlled access, they are simply not OA.

The virtues of green OA are that it (theoretically) doesn't require consent or change in policies from publishers; that—up to a point—it doesn't change the current model; that it might be cheaper to implement than full-scale gold OA (depending on the actual cost of establishing and maintaining effective repositories); and that it might yield easier and more comprehensive searching if there are search engines doing exhaustive harvesting.

The chief drawbacks include one of the virtues: Green OA does not inherently change the current subscription model and won't provide near-term cost savings for libraries. Green OA also doesn't necessarily provide the final version of journal articles, which may make the OA version less useful and certainly not a clear substitute for the published version. There are other issues, discussed later, having to do with effective access and long-term access.

As of mid-2010, most traditional journals allow green OA in one form or another. I've seen a number as high as 90% of traditional journals, although the percentage that allows immediate deposit of postprints is considerably smaller.

Nobody knows how many articles are available through green OA. The OAIster database (founded by the University of Michigan, now part of OCLC) includes more than 25 million records from more than 1,100 contributors. Those records are freely searchable as part of Worldcat.org, but also through a separate OAIster-only engine at http://oaister.worldcat.org. The 25 million records include many things other than journal articles, and problems with repository software can result in things like having one OAIster record for each page of a scanned book. Additionally, some OAIster records point to items that turn out not to be open access—in one small random sample, only about one-quarter of the records led to true OA materials.[2] Still, OAIster (and other OAI harvests) provide clear demonstrations that green OA can be effective OA. ScientificCommons, www.scientificcommons.org, shows more than 38 million "publications" from 1,269 repositories as of September 23, 2010. That figure presumably includes gold as well as green OA, just as Google Scholar includes many sources of material.

Gold OA

Gold open access—sometimes called "the gold road to open access"—means the journal itself provides immediate full-text online access at no charge to readers. The online version of peer-reviewed portions of gold OA journals are funded by some means other than mandatory subscriptions.

Gold OA requires OA journals: journals that provide immediate, free online access to peer-reviewed articles. *Journal* is a slightly trickier term today than it was in, say, 1985—but before we consider that, here's Peter Suber's terse description of OA journals, also from "A Very Brief Introduction . . .":

> OA journals perform peer review and then make the approved contents freely available to the world. Their expenses consist of peer review, manuscript preparation, and server space. OA journals pay their bills very much the way broadcast television and radio stations do: those with an interest in disseminating the content pay the production costs upfront so that access can be free of charge for everyone with the right equipment. Sometimes this means that journals have a subsidy from the hosting university or professional society. Sometimes it means that journals charge a processing fee on accepted articles, to be paid by the author or the author's sponsor (employer, funding agency). OA journals that charge processing fees usually waive them in cases of economic hardship. OA journals with institutional subsidies tend to charge no processing fees. OA journals can get by on lower subsidies or fees if they have income from other publications, advertising, priced add-ons, or auxiliary services. Some institutions and consortia arrange fee discounts. Some OA publishers waive the fee for all researchers affiliated with institutions that have purchased an annual membership. There's a lot of room for creativity in finding ways to pay the costs of a peer-

reviewed OA journal, and we're far from having exhausted our clever-
ness and imagination.

While this paragraph provides an excellent summary of key aspects and possibilities
for OA journals, some items deserve discussion and amplification. For example:

- An effective OA journal requires publicity—so authors and readers
  alike know that it exists and why they should pay attention to it—and
  website maintenance, which can be nontrivial expenses.
- Processing fees—typically charged for accepted articles, not submitted
  articles—are frequently called *author fees*, and Gold OA is sometimes
  called *author-pays publishing*. Both terms are misleading, the latter
  one particularly so and frequently used as an implicit argument
  against gold OA. A better term is *author-side fees*, since processing
  fees will increasingly come from funding agencies or institutional
  memberships rather than from authors themselves. The bigger
  problem with author-pays publishing is that it's not true for most OA
  journals.
- Most OA journals don't charge author-side fees—and many traditional
  journals (called *toll access* in some OA discussions) do charge author-
  side fees. Some studies have found that a higher percentage of
  traditional journals than OA journals charge author-side fees. As with
  many comments about numbers, these statements are tricky, since a
  journal can publish anywhere from half a dozen to many thousand
  articles each year. It's not clear what percentage of OA publishing—
  that is, what percentage of articles published in OA journals—involves
  author-side fees, just as it's not clear whether the percentage of
  traditionally published articles with author-side fees is higher than the
  percentage of OA-published articles with author-side fees.
- Note "other publications," "priced add-ons" and "auxiliary
  services" in the definitional paragraph. There is no requirement or
  expectation that an OA journal will be free in its entirety or in all
  forms. Some OA journals charge online subscriptions for a variety
  of non-peer-reviewed material, such as book reviews, news from
  the field, summary reports and other value-added services. Even for
  peer-reviewed articles, while online access must be wholly free and
  open for the journal to be legitimately OA, there is no requirement
  or expectation that a print version of the journal will be free. Many
  OA journals don't have print versions, but some do, at reasonable
  subscription fees. A few are using print-on-demand or publish-
  on-demand services such as Lulu to make print editions (issues or
  volumes) available only as needed, typically for little more than
  the cost of production. Examples include the *Journal of Industrial
  Engineering and Management* and *Journal of Stuttering Therapy, Advocacy
  and Research*.

The virtues of gold OA are that it assures immediate access to final articles, with all copyediting and other manuscript preparation in place, and that it should lower costs for libraries to the extent that OA journals displace traditional journals or traditional journals transform to OA journals.

The main drawback of gold OA is that it directly challenges existing journal publishers and the existing publishing system—and does no good for library budgets until and unless OA journals displace traditional journals.

As of mid-2010, roughly 20% of peer-reviewed journals are OA, if we accept the assertion that there are about 25,000 peer-reviewed journals. The *Directory of Open Access Journals* lists more than 5,400 journals as of September 2010. Naturally, 20% of journals does not equal 20% of articles. A study published in *PLoS One*, an innovative gold OA journal (www.plosone.org), on June 23, 2010 finds that 20.4% of a sample of peer-reviewed articles published in 2008 are available openly in full text on the web—but only 8.5% are available at publisher sites; the rest are accessible through search engines and appear in repositories or other sites.[3] At this point, and with singular exceptions such as *PLoS One*, OA journals tend to publish fewer articles than traditional journals, hardly surprising given the newness of most OA journals. It's worth noting that the article cites a typical one-year embargo as the basis for studying 2008 articles in early 2010: the 20% figure for articles is for delayed OA, not full OA. It's also worth noting that one-third of the green OA articles were not in repositories but rather on personal websites or other websites, which are less likely to remain available for the long term.

According to *The stm report*, an October 2009 overview published by the International Association of Scientific, Technical and Medical Publishers available at www.stm-assoc .org/2009_10_13_MWC_STM_Report.pdf, only about 2% of a claimed 1.5 million articles published per year are published in "full" OA journals, with another 5% in journals offering delayed access and 1% published in hybrid journals (subscription journals that offer OA only for articles where a special author-side fee is paid). That's a snapshot, and the percentage of articles in gold OA journals will certainly increase.

Other Colors

You'll see mention of other colors in some discussions of OA, but with no broad agreement or usage. While there could be other OA vehicles—e.g., personal websites, blogs, wikis, etc.—there are no agreed standards for such vehicles and much less likelihood of broad, well-defined searchability or longevity. (For more on the longevity question, see chapter 3.)

Tom Wilson, publisher and editor of the long-established OA journal *Information Research*, further distinguishes between what he calls *partial* open access journals and *true* open access journals, reserving the latter label for journals that don't have author-side fees. He also calls these journals, funded by subsidies, voluntary work, grants, or advertising, *platinum access* journals.

Gratis OA

Gratis OA is online digital literature that anyone can read without charge. There are no price barriers to read the literature. You'll also see "weak OA" used, particularly prior to mid-2008, when Peter Suber began using the terms *gratis* and *libre*.

The very existence of gratis OA and the perceived need to define the term indicate the reality: the Budapest, Bethesda, and Berlin statements require an ideal set of conditions—conditions that many scholars and journals find difficult to meet. This is a classic case where the best can be the enemy of the good. Requiring all the conditions defined in the key OA statements would substantially delay and reduce the availability of journal articles to be read freely, a key objective and the one of most importance to most researchers, practitioners, and users. The bulk of the problems addressed by OA, and *all* of the problems apparent to perhaps 99% of potential users, are covered by gratis OA—the ability to read freely gets us most of the way there.

If you're familiar with Creative Commons licenses, you can summarize gratis OA by saying that even the most restrictive CC license, BY-NC-ND, supports gratis OA: You can read it (and copy it for others to read), but not much more. In practice, if there's no CC license on an OA source, it may not even be legal to copy articles for preservation purposes, substantially weakening long-term access.

Libre OA

Libre OA is online digital literature that is free of charge and free of "unnecessary" copyright and licensing restrictions. You'll also see "strong OA" used prior to mid-2008.

I would say that libre OA is what Budapest, Bethesda, and Berlin call open access—but it's not that simple. *Unnecessary* is a tricky term. For example:

- Some authors are happy to support derivative use—data mining and the like—but unwilling to see their articles reused in commercial publications or on commercial websites without permission and possible payment. In Creative Commons terms, these authors would use BY-NC licenses.
- Some authors or journals might only provide online access to articles precisely as published, by providing them in PDF form. While the author or journal might not impose explicit restrictions, PDF can and frequently does impose a barrier to most derivative uses unless it's possible to extract the text from the PDF (which depends on how it was generated and what permissions were set).
- Technically, even the Creative Commons BY requirement may present a barrier to reuse: would text-mining operations inherently assure that writers are credited for their words?

Another way to look at gratis and libre is in terms of barriers. Gratis OA removes pricing barriers for use of the journal literature. Libre OA removes at least some permission barriers from those wishing to use articles in ways beyond reading and copying them. Unless the only remaining restriction on reuse is the requirement for attribution, libre OA may be a misnomer—but that's probably too restrictive. As Peter Suber puts it, "Some OA providers permit commercial reuse and some do not. Some permit derivative works and some do not." If you're not permitting commercial reuse or derivative works, it's hard to see what permission barriers you're removing—why this form of OA belongs in the libre camp at all. Maybe we need *full libre OA* as a term that means all permission barriers, possibly excepting some form of attribution, have been removed.

Currently, it appears that most OA literature—whether green OA or gold OA—is gratis or somewhere between gratis and libre. The differences between gratis and libre primarily involve secondary uses of published material, including data mining. So, for example:

- If you're preparing a textbook or any commercial product, you should be able to use libre OA articles but you'll probably need to ask permission to use gratis OA articles.
- If you want to do data mining, some gratis OA articles won't be available, either because they carry restrictions on reuse or because they're in forms (e.g., PDF) that may not support data mining.

Combining the Colors and Flavors

Libre OA must be gratis OA—it's not possible for it to be otherwise. Gold OA should be green OA, but that's not a requirement. It's possible for a journal to make its articles freely readable at time of publication but not allow those articles to be deposited in institutional or subject repositories. (It is certainly the case that some OA journals ask that articles not be made available in repositories *prior* to formal publication.) There's a (weak) economic case for doing that if a gold OA journal is partially or wholly supported by web advertising, as refusal to allow green OA assures that all readers come through the journal's own website to maximize page views and related ad revenue. (That's a hypothetical. I am not personally aware of any gold OA journals that do, in fact, restrict green OA after publication.)

Gray Areas

What do you call a journal that makes peer-reviewed articles available for free online reading—but only after six months or a year? What do you call a subject repository where articles *must* be deposited—but where free online access can be embargoed for up to a year?

John Willinsky calls the former *delayed open access*. The National Institutes of Health (NIH) calls the latter PubMed, and most would consider PubMed one of the great examples of open access at work.

In both cases, it seems reasonable to call these good steps in the right direction—but not true OA. Timeliness is important to truly effective use of existing research, and timeliness may be critical for a lay reader who needs to understand important new medical findings.

Delayed situations are compromises, just as gratis OA and the weak definition of libre OA are compromises. It's important to recognize compromises for what they are: necessary steps to improve existing situations, but steps that don't quite reach the desired conclusion.

Free Online Scholarship (FOS)

You may see this term used in 20th-century discussions of open access issues, and you'll see the abbreviation in the URL for many key documents. Peter Suber used this term for some time prior to the Budapest declaration—since steps toward open access go back long before 2002, to at least 1966.

Other Opens

There are many other catchprases beginning with "open." Dorothea Salo provides the slides from a June 2010 presentation entitled "Open Sesame! (and other open movements)" at www.slideshare.net/cavlec/open-sesame-and-other-open-movements. Her list includes open source (software for which human-readable source code is freely available), open standards, open content (e.g., the free culture movement), open courseware, open data, and open notebook science—and that's a tiny (but useful) subset of the Opens.

This report doesn't deal with other Opens. When you encounter an Open term, dig a little: *Open* can be used for commercial and propriety efforts as easily as it can for commendable efforts to improve science, software and humanity through shared resources.

BEYOND THE PRIMARY TERMS

Portions of chapter 3 and chapter 4 discuss some of the things that open access is not. For example, it is not an assertion that scholarly publishing involves no costs; it is not a movement against copyright law; it is not a movement against peer review.

The term *royalty-free literature* has been used to define the primary target for open access, but it may not be the right term. After all, most magazine articles and newspaper articles are royalty free: the writer receives a single payment, either as a salary or as an article fee. (In the latter case, the writer also typically retains copyright and the rights to reuse the material for other purposes after some reasonable period.) The OA movement has not, to my knowledge, involved the suggestion that magazine articles and newspaper articles ought to be freely available online. Unfortunately, there's not a good terse term. *Payment free* doesn't work, because scholars are most certainly paid to write peer-reviewed articles, as such articles are the most visible outcomes of research. The key is that *publishers* don't pay scholars for the articles, and that's hard to sum up in a terse phrase.

OA can and does go beyond peer-reviewed articles, but such articles are the focus of most OA activity and the area where libraries can see the most potential benefit from widespread adoption of OA.

NOTES

1. Peter Suber, Open Access Overview, 2010, www.earlham.edu/~peters/fos/overview.htm.
2. Personal communication from Dorothea Salo, September 2010.
3. Bo Christer Björk, Patrik Welling, Mikael Laakso1, Peter Majlender, Turid Hedlund, Guðni Guðnason, "Open Access to the Scientific Journal Literature: Situation 2009," *PLoS One* 5(6) (June 23, 2010).

3

ISSUES FOR
OPEN ACCESS

Open access offers clear advantages for citizens, libraries, researchers, and authors. So why don't we have 100% open access—or at least more than 20% open access?

The obvious answer is that things don't change that rapidly. The traditional journal system has grown over a couple of centuries. Replacing that system with a different and, in some ways, more complex system couldn't happen overnight.

What was probably the first free peer-reviewed online journal, *New Horizons in Adult Education*, began in fall 1987 (it's noteworthy that this journal is still publishing, with four issues in 2009). While not a journal, the *Newsletter on Serials Pricing Issues*—the first real attempt at ongoing examination of the serials crisis—began in 1989. And arXiv, the longest-established subject repository (beginning with physics and adding some other scientific fields), was launched in 1991. I'd consider those as starting dates for three key drivers of OA: online-only journals with no subscription charges, paying attention to the increasing problems of the traditional journal system, and robust online repositories. I'm not sure you could call those three steps a movement, however, and even if you do, that makes the movement somewhere between 19 and 23 years old.

What steps could be considered the start of a movement? That's harder to say, but these might be considered clear candidates:

- The September 98 Forum, founded and still moderated by Stevan Harnad (it later became the American Scientist Open Access Forum), began in August 1998.
- The Open Archives Initiative began in 1999.
- The Budapest conference took place in December 2001 and issued its statement in February 2002—the same month that the University of Michigan founded OAIster, a search engine harvesting OAI repositories. Three months later, Lawrence Lessig launched Creative Commons and Peter Suber started the FOS News blog (later Open Access News).

I think it's reasonable to suggest that OA as a movement dates back less than a decade, even though incidents along the way date back another decade. Or maybe longer: the first entries in the "Timeline of the open access movement"—as maintained at http://oad.simmons.edu/oadwiki/Timeline—are from 1966, when the U.S. Department of Education launched ERIC and the National Library of Medicine launched Medline. But Medline wasn't free until 1997, so it's hard to count that.

It's hard to dislodge two centuries of practice in a decade of experimentation, particularly when, for most of the people who would need to change, existing practice seemed to be working pretty well. From that perspective, achieving 20% open access may be a victory.

Inertia and invisibility are two major ongoing issues for open access. People tend to do in the present what they've done in the past, and for most researchers and scholars, access and pricing have been relatively invisible issues. We'll touch on those again, but those certainly aren't the only issues for open access. This chapter considers a range of issues that make OA difficult to achieve rapidly and completely. Some are problems that need solving; some are issues that need to be addressed. (The difference between a problem and an issue? Problems have solutions; issues don't.)

Note the distinction between chapter 3 and chapter 4. Chapter 4 considers *controversies*—some legitimate, some myths spread to preserve the traditional model. Controversies are also problems for OA, to be sure. This chapter focuses on cases that don't appear to be controversial (except to publishers trying to stave off any movement toward OA) but that do require attention. Since large portions of this chapter are about issues for OA journals and, separately, issues for OA repositories, it's important to note that "one road or both?" is an ongoing controversy—at least to some within the OA community—that appears in chapter 4. Peer review does *not* appear in this chapter, because doubts about peer review for OA journals fall into the deliberate (and fallacious) controversy category.

ISSUES FOR OA JOURNALS

What *is* an open access journal? The definitions can be fuzzy. I would say that an OA journal publishes peer-reviewed articles that are all made available for reading and redistribution free, online, immediately upon publication. But it's not that simple.

What Defines an OA Journal?

The Directory of Open Access Journals (*DOAJ*, at www.doaj.org) includes more than 5,400 journals as of September 2010—but *DOAJ*'s definition is "free, full text, quality controlled scientific and scholarly journals." In other words, a journal that uses "editorial quality control" rather than peer review may be eligible for *DOAJ* if it allows users to "read, download, copy, distribute, print, search, or link to the full texts" of articles.

What's a journal? *DOAJ* says a journal is intended to appear indefinitely at regular intervals, generally more frequently than annually, with numbered or dated issues. That's tricky, as it would appear to exclude some alternative approaches to peer-reviewed online publishing:

- There are OA "journals" that don't define issues at all, instead posting articles to a site as they're approved. (*DOAJ*'s own guide for starting OA journals says, "Many Open Access journals are not published with issues.")

- There's no good reason an OA journal couldn't appear annually, particularly if it's an overlay journal—a case where articles are posted as approved, with "issues" consisting of organized sets of pointers issued as digital tables of contents.

DOAJ defines journals as things "that report primary results of research or overviews of research results to a scholarly community." The last four words seem pointlessly limiting. Is *Science* less of a journal because many of its 130,000 print subscribers are lay readers?

There's another oddity about *DOAJ*'s criteria: while content must be freely available without delay, free registration as a requirement for reading is acceptable. That's a barrier, albeit a low one. Ideally, you should not need to register to read an OA article. On the other hand, *DOAJ* says, "All content should be available in full text"—a requirement that goes beyond OA, which requires that only peer-reviewed articles be available freely in full text. Since one funding method for OA journals is added services provided for a price, this requirement seems to be in conflict with the broader aims of OA.

It may be useful to divide OA journals into three subsets:

Born OA: Journals that have made all peer-reviewed articles available online for free reading and redistribution since the beginning of the journal.

Hybrid OA: Subscription-based journals in which some articles are free, usually because author-side fees have been paid, and others are not free or free only on a delayed basis. The "author section" of *DOAJ* includes "& Hybrid" after "Open Access" in the name of the directory—and that section does include hybrid OA journals. So, for example, *DOAJ* proper lists 191 journals on languages and literatures—but the author's list includes 197 journals, including six flagged as hybrid journals.

Turned OA: Journals that began as subscription journals or with other forms of controlled access (e.g., controlled circulation journals or journals distributed solely to association members) and have converted to OA.

DOAJ shows journals going back to 1915. Given that the first "born OA" journal (as far as I can determine) appeared in 1987, it's clear that "turned OA" journals exist and are significant for the future of OA.

Some of the issues here are issues *for* OA journals, worth considering by librarians because some libraries are (and more should be) OA publishers themselves. Others are issues *about* OA journals as they relate to library needs.

Can OA Journals Be Competitive?

Until recently, this might have been the biggest issue for OA journals. Can OA journals compete for articles with the best of the subscription journals? Will they be viewed as competitive—which, today, means having high *impact factors* (an astonishingly sloppy measure of a journal's impact, but one that's easy to find and has yet to be replaced by better measures).

Peter Suber points out one problem in his "Ten challenges for open access journals"[1]—a long article that should be compulsory reading if you're considering new OA journals.

Impact factors (IF) discriminate against newer journals because Thomson Scientific doesn't calculate IF for journals less than two years old—and many OA journals were founded recently. For that matter, Thomson calculates IF for less than one-third of published scholarly journals.

Now, thanks to the Public Library of Science (PLoS) and some other publishers, the answer to this question is clear. In the 2008 Journal Citation Reports, five OA journals—four of them from *PLoS*—had the highest IF in their fields. Those aren't all niche journals: *PLoS Biology* had the highest IF of 71 ranked journals in this key field.

OA journals can be competitive—but only by maintaining quality and doing enough marketing and other publicity to make sure authors and readers know they exist and offer high-quality outlets. It's still an issue, particularly for the 90% (or more) of OA journals that do not yet have IFs.

Can OA Journals Survive and Thrive?

The simplest answer may be the best one: pointing out OA journals that have lasted for quite a long time and OA publishers that are stable and even profitable.

But it's not that simple. Many experiments in OA publishing did *not* survive, particularly in the early years of "try it and see what happens" journals with implicit institutional subsidies as their only source of funding.

I studied pioneer OA journals in 2001 and 2006. The initial study was entitled "Getting Past the Arc of Enthusiasm" because I suspected some early experiments would fit a pattern of starting out strong and fading away after two or three years, a pattern I call "the arc of enthusiasm."[2] I focused on *very* early experiments: a directory of 104 free refereed electronic journals that began in 1995 or before. It turns out that only 86 of the 104 were, in fact, free refereed journals in 1995, and 57% of those (49) were still publishing in 2001. (Of the other 43%, just over half fit the "arc of enthusiasm" pattern.)

When I prepared the 2001 article, I suggested a definition for "lasting" journal titles, given the reality that few things last forever, including subscription journals as well as OA journals. I asserted that a journal that lasted six years could be considered successful even if it later disappeared. I continue to think that's a reasonable starting point. By that standard, just under two-thirds of the early OA experiments were successes.

I looked at the situation again in 2006, in "Pioneer OA journals: The arc of enthusiasm, five years later."[3] In the process, I discovered that 3 of the 86 pioneers actually began publishing after 1995, even though they were listed in a 1995 directory. The good news is that, while eleven pioneer OA journals (all of which lasted for at least six years) had stopped publishing by 2006, 41 were still publishing in 2006. All of those had been publishing for at least a decade, with some going back even farther.

But the 1995 list I worked from was incomplete. Checking *DOAJ* in early September 2006, I encountered 189 additional journals that were still publishing as of 2006 with initial publication dates of 1995 or earlier. The October 2006 *Cites & Insights* includes details on each of these. My summary conclusion is that nearly half of them clearly were OA at least since 1995, with most of the rest either unclear or having provided retrospective access to earlier articles after converting to OA.

I won't get into funding issues here. There are many ways to fund an OA journal, and fewer than half of current OA journals rely on author-side fees for funding. Some journals continue to be funded by implicit subsidies, including at least one journal in library and information science (*Information Research*, http://informationr.net/ir, which began in 1995–96 and is now in its 15th volume). We need to know more about how OA journals are funded and what funding methods work best, but there's not enough known to attempt a summary here.

Hybrid Journals and the Transition to OA

Hybrid journals—ones where articles are OA if additional author-side fees have been paid—may serve as ways for subscription publishers to test the water. They may also be questionable cases, when extremely high author-side fees are set ($5,000 in at least one case): if nobody pays the fee, the publisher can say, "See? Nobody really wants OA."

Legitimate hybrid journals set reasonable author-side fees and, equally important, adjust subscription prices based on the percentage of OA articles in the previous year. Ideally, such journals will eventually make the transition to full OA. That's not unheard of: Molecular Diversity Preservation International converted four hybrid journals to full OA in 2007—and, two years later, reported that the conversion seems to have yielded higher impact factors.

Society Publishers and Subsidized Operations

Most professional societies publish journals, most of them peer reviewed. Many societies use profits from journal subscriptions to subsidize other society functions, and some societies have turned over their journals to commercial publishers. Some society publishers are among the harshest critics of open access, and some complain that open access would eliminate the profits currently yielded from high prices for subscription journals.

I count this as an issue because there should be no controversy. I can think of no ethical or moral reason to expect academic libraries to support scholarly associations other than, possibly, ACRL or a state library association. In all other cases, library subscriptions are covert subsidies, taking money from a library's acquisition budget to subsidize a specific nonlibrary group.

The worthiness of these societies does not give them license to raid library budgets. If they require subsidies, those subsidies should come directly from appropriate departments of institutions, either through higher dues for association members or through direct institutional support of the associations.

Lumping All Subscription Journals Together

The end point for the OA movement is for all peer-reviewed articles to be available online with no fees. At that point, it's hard to believe there would be subscription revenue for most journals other than charges related to auxiliary services or provision of print copies.

Some publishers, including quite a few scholarly society publishers, complain that they've become targets even though their journals are modestly priced. Some scholarly societies charge little more than production costs for journal subscriptions. It's not unreasonable for a publisher asking $60 for a year's subscription to object to being lumped in with a journal that costs $30,000. The small guys or, rather, the publishers with modest prices may seem like easy targets, but they're not the most important targets.

Heather Morrison offers an example in the library field in "On the wide disparity in publisher cost-efficiency," a June 17, 2010 post at *The Imaginary Journal of Poetic Economics* (http://poeticeconomics.blogspot.com). She says, "It it not fair . . . to treat the mission-oriented publisher that has never charged more than they needed to survive, as if they were the same as the highly for-profit publishers." Her example (using Canadian dollars): *Library Management* from Emerald costs $14,600 for an institutional subscription. *College and Research Libraries* from ACRL costs at most $80 for an institutional subscription, and that's outside the U.S. and Canada (where it's $70 or $75, respectively). A more directly comparable journal might be *Library Leadership & Management* from LLAMA—and it costs at most $95 ($85 in the U.S., Canada, and Mexico). Morrison argues that *C&RL* is more prestigious than *Library Management*, and I would argue the same for *LL&M*—and yet, both of the ALA divisional journals together cost less than 1.2% of the for-profit journal. That may be an extreme case, but differentials of ten to one aren't uncommon.

John Willinsky cites a study of economics journals done in 2001 that makes much the same point. The average subscription price for commercial journals among the 20 top-ranked journals (by impact factor) was $1,660; the average for nonprofit journals was $180. All five of the top five journals were from nonprofits. By the standards of some science, technology, and medicine journals, $1,660 is chump change, but you could still get nine nonprofit journals for the price of one commercial journal. There are nonprofits that charge extremely high prices—and those should be early targets just as much as overpriced commercial journals.

Bad Pennies: The Problem of OA Entrepreneurs

Is gold OA a scam? Absolutely not. That's not a controversy. Anyone who suggests that all OA journals are scams is being deliberately dishonest. For one thing, most OA journals don't have author-side fees, and it's hard to see how a scam can make sense if it's not charging.

Are *some* OA publishers scammers? Apparently so—and that's not so much a controversy as an issue, one that probably won't disappear. Jeffrey Beall's "'Predatory' open-access scholarly publishers" in the April 2010 *Charleston Advisor* names more than half a dozen publishers with questionable practices. (Unfortunately, the article—once apparently OA—now costs $38 to view; you'll find a list of suspect publishers from the article in a May 19, 2010, post with the same title at *Journalology*, http://journalology .blogspot.com.) These publishers seem to be author-fee magnets with little or no peer review and no apparent concern for long-term access.

How do you spot a scam operation? There are several red flags:

- A publisher initiates dozens of new OA titles at once.
- "Published" titles don't appear to have any, or many, papers.
- The publisher sends e-mail to large numbers of researchers asking them to submit papers or to join editorial boards.
- The publisher conceals the names of editors or editorial board members.

- The business address for the publisher is not verifiable.
- There's little evidence of peer review.

If people listed as editorial board members indicate that they've never engaged in peer review for the journal or, worse, have never *heard* of the journal, that's a pretty clear indication.

There's now an association for open access, the Open Access Scholarly Publishers Association (OASPA, www.oaspa.org). It maintains a code of conduct for OA publishers and has a screening process for new members and procedures to handle complaints against OA publishers. As of early August 2010, 15 professional publishing organizations belong to OASPA, as do 14 scientist/scholar publishers, four other voting organizations, and two dozen associate members. While these are early years, the association should help to assure quality standards for OA journals.

Have there been scams within subscription journal publishing? Absolutely. Not only have there been publishers who preannounce journals, take subscription fees, then never publish the journals (possibly reimbursing subscription fees but gaining interest along the way), there have been pseudo-journals published by large international publishers to serve the interests of special groups, selectively republishing existing articles in an effort to make a particular case.

Is Partial Open Access Good Enough?
In *The Access Principle*, John Willinsky offers "ten flavors of open access to journal articles." The ten include

1. home pages
2. "e-print archives" (institutional and subject repositories)
3. author fees
4. subsidized (gold OA journals supported through some form of subsidy)
5. "dual-mode" (journals that charge for print but not for online access)
6. delayed
7. partial (journals that offer access to *some* articles)
8. "per capita" (third-world OA through registered institution)
9. indexing (access only to bibliographic information and abstracts)
10. cooperative arrangements

Most OA advocates would assert that delayed, partial and indexing are not flavors of open access—they are business as usual. For that matter, some OA advocates would argue that papers deposited on home pages aren't truly open access, as they may lack not only proper metadata for harvesting but also any real semblance of long-term stability. (They may also violate publisher agreements and even be illegal in some cases.)

I would argue that, of Willinsky's ten flavors, only the second through fifth and tenth flavors are legitimate OA—that home page access, delayed access, partial access, access only through registered institutions, and most of all, access that stops with abstracts do not deserve the term *open access*. But is this a case where the better (true OA) is the enemy of the good, or where "good" simply isn't good enough?

Are Journals the Right Media?

This may not be an OA issue at all, but it's one that pops up from time to time. You could phrase this another way: have journals and traditional peer review outlived their usefulness?

Alternative suggestions have included posting articles as blog posts, with comments and linkbacks used as a form of peer review, or depositing articles to repositories and counting on postpublication review to identify good and worthless (or defective) articles. They're not new suggestions; for example, proposals to scrap journals and use links as a form of refereeing date from as early as 2002. So far, none of these suggestions has gained much traction. There are experiments, however. For example, *Shakespeare Quarterly* posted four essays that had not yet been accepted online, gathered online signed comments (from 41 people in all) visible to the authors and, after author revisions, accepted the essays following editorial review.

One very successful OA journal may have changed the issue. One aspect of traditional journal publication is "importance"—the fact that some very selective journals review articles not just for scientific validity but also for whether they're "important" enough for this particular journal. By contrast, *PLoS One*, with a much lower processing fee than other PLoS journals (but still one that, at $1,500, needs some justification), reviews only for technically validity, not for whether the article is sufficiently important. *PLoS One* (which has no paper counterpart) publishes rapidly and voluminously: for example, when checked on August 8, 2010, 103 articles had been published in the past week. It's now clear that significant articles are appearing in *PLoS One*.

ISSUES FOR OA REPOSITORIES

Some OA advocates assert that every academic institution should have an OA repository—and a fair number of OA repositories are founded and administered within academic libraries.

The Real Cost of OA Repositories

What does it actually cost to run an OA repository? Stevan Harnad says it costs almost nothing: you just need a server, free software, and a few hours of a technician's time to set it up. Some of those who operate OA repositories would say it costs a small fortune to run an *effective* OA repository—for example, an ARL study found that, for these very large university libraries, the mean cost of IR implementation was more than $180,000 and the mean annual cost of operation was more than $110,000.

As with journals, there's no single answer. Yes, an institution can set up a repository for little more than the cost of a high-end PC, say a few thousand dollars. Will such a repository survive and thrive? That's a tougher question. A bit of the truth may come from Les Carr, repository manager at the University of Southampton, Harnad's institution. In a blog post about repositories and other services, he ended with this sentence: "Repositories are hard work because changing researchers' working practices is hard work and I guess there's no single magic solution that's going to make that effort disappear!"

Consider some of the work involved in populating a repository, getting campus scholars to make their articles available in suitable form, including new articles and (ideally) previously published articles:

- Convincing faculty and other scholars, on an ongoing basis, that depositing their articles is worthwhile.
- Helping them understand and negotiate author addenda to publisher agreements so there's no issue of legality for deposited articles.
- Making sure articles are deposited in a useful form and the metadata meets OAI standards.
- Assuring the long-term health of the repository: making sure it won't disappear in some campus reorganization.

Institutional, Subject, or Other?

Should OA repositories be institutional, subject based, or based on other criteria? ArXiv is enormously successful as a subject-based archive primarily focused on physics (at least until recently), and PubMed, already important, will continue to grow in size and importance, aided by NIH's mandate for deposit. There are also millions of refereed articles in OAI-compliant institutional repositories and will be millions more.

It's not a zero-sum game, and it's not an either/or proposition. The same article can legitimately appear on the site of a gold OA journal, in a subject repository, and on the repository of each author's institution—and, quite possibly, on a series of other repositories using LOCKSS-style software to assure longevity and access.

LONGEVITY, PRESERVATION AND ACCESS

When an article becomes available via green or gold OA, it's available to anyone with Internet access today—but what about a year, ten years, a century from now? OA does nothing to assure long-term access, except to the extent that Creative Commons BY or BY-NC licenses encourage other sites to replicate OA articles.

Dead Links and Abandoned Sites

As I was preparing this chapter, I went to check a document on the costs of institutional repositories. The link yielded a 404 message: the page was no longer there. Since the link didn't include a title, I couldn't do a title search. This happens to all of us. Sites disappear and are reorganized; in the process, links die. At one point, it was estimated that the half-life of a URL was 90 days. This isn't a theoretical issue for open access journals. For at least ten pioneering online journals, issues have disappeared from the visible Internet.

My own e-journal, *Cites & Insights*, is not a scholarly journal: it does not publish peer-reviewed scholarly articles. It may be a prime example of what can happen with journals that lack solid institutional backing. On two occasions, the URL for the journal (and the site on which the journal is housed) has changed—once because a university site was offered and the personal webpage used for the first year or two was running out of room, a second time because the university site was no longer available. In both cases, although all issues of the journal were moved to the new site, hundreds—and in the second case, thousands—of links were and are defunct. When I stop publishing the e-journal, I may prepay for several years' hosting on its current site—but, come death or long-term disinterest, that site will also disappear. The same may very well be true for many small OA publishers, just as it's true for small or failing subscription publishers.

In my case, there's a solution for access, although not for links: an institutional archive is mirroring issues as they're published, and that institutional archive seems likely to be around for decades to come. Similar solutions need to be in place for OA journals, especially the smallest and least institutional-backed OA journals.

Improving Chances for Long-Term Access

Perhaps the most vulnerable in terms of long-term access are small OA journal publishers, some of them no more than part of a person's time in a university or other service. Will those articles be accessible in a decade? In a century?

DOAJ is working with the National Library of the Netherlands on one project for long-term preservation of OA journals. Three paragraphs from the *DOAJ* site, from the section on long-term archiving, help define the problem and what they're doing:

> Long-term preservation of scholarly publications is of major importance for the research community. New formats of scholarly publications, new business models and new ways of dissemination are constantly being developed. To secure permanent access to scientific output for the future, focused on the preservation of articles published in open access journals, a cooperation between Directory of Open Access Journals (*DOAJ*-www.doaj.org), developed and operated by Lund University Libraries and the e-Depot of the National Library of the Netherlands (www.kb.nl/e-depot-en), has been initiated.

> The composition of the *DOAJ* collection (currently 4000 journals) is characterized by a very large number of publishers (2.000+), each publishing a very small number of journals on different platforms, in different formats and in more than 50 different languages. Many of these publishers are—with a number of exceptions—fragile when it comes to financial, technical and administrative sustainability.

> At present *DOAJ* and KB carry out a pilot project aimed at setting up a workflow for processing open access journals listed with *DOAJ*. In the pilot a limited number of open access journals will be subject to long term preservation. These activities will be scaled up shortly and long term archiving of the journals listed in the *DOAJ* at KB's e-Depot will become an integral part of the service provided by the *DOAJ*.

Apparent easy solutions don't always work. The Internet Archive is far from complete and can only be searched by URL. Cooperative solutions such as LOCKSS require up-front work by publishers and libraries to establish archiving. When a journal moves—or when a parent institution reorganizes—URLs can change without notification or redirection, stranding links. Digital preservation efforts by libraries involve legal issues and require long-term institutional commitments. You can almost assume that hundreds of smaller OA journals will disappear without a trace—just as hundreds or thousands of smaller subscription journals have vanished over the decades.

OA Does Not Provide Universal Access

It's worth making the point that OA itself doesn't provide universal access, for several reasons. Peter Suber points out four of them in his "Open Access overview":[4]

1. *Filtering and censorship barriers.* Many schools, employers and governments want to limit what you can see.

2. *Language barriers.* Most online literature is in English, or just one language, and machine translation is very weak.

3. *Handicap access barriers.* Most web sites are not yet as accessible to handicapped users as they should be.

4. *Connectivity barriers.* The digital divide keeps billions of people, including millions of serious scholars, offline.

There are no perfect solutions. OA brings us about as far as any one development can—to the extent that we achieve broad adoption of OA.

ISSUES FOR LIBRARY USE OF OA

Let's look at a few issues that relate more specifically to libraries as OA users than to journals and repositories as such.

Searchability and Access

Are articles in OA journals—and the green OA versions of articles in subscription journals—as visible to your users as articles for which they or your library must pay for access?

That's a tough question, although the answer should certainly be yes. Realistically, libraries can fall into a typical trap: that for which you pay is regarded as more valuable than that for which you don't pay. If you're paying hundreds of thousands or millions of dollars a year for full-text aggregations (essentially online subscription journals in aggregated form), you're going to make sure those articles are fully indexed and searchable. If you build aggregated search systems, you'll be certain those articles are represented.

Are you taking as much care with the 5,400 journals (so far) and millions of articles you don't have to pay for? Are those articles fully represented in your aggregated search systems, or must users be aware of systems such as OAIster and remember to use them? If a patron finds an article that's available for $30 or via ILL, are your systems set up so you can be reasonably certain that article isn't also available, for free, from an OA repository?

If not, OA works at a disadvantage—as do your patrons.

Open Access and the Big Deal

At this point, chances are that about 20% of the articles you're paying for in your Big Deals are also available for free from OA sources. But you're still paying for the Big Deals, probably with annual price increases in excess of inflation.

What happens when 40% of the articles are available in OA form? What about 60%? At what point can, or should, the availability of OA versions serve as a lever for libraries to get lower prices for Big Deals, or encourage libraries to abandon such deals altogether?

I have no answers, but it's something academic librarians should be paying attention to. And it relates directly to the last library-related issue discussed in this chapter:

When Will Libraries See Savings?

I started writing about open access (before that term was used) because I'm a humanities person, and I saw that humanities in general and books in particular were getting squeezed out of academic library acquisitions budget as libraries continued a vain attempt to keep paying for subscription-based scholarly journals. It struck me then, and strikes me now, that the systemic costs of OA journals should be far less than the actual prices (which are by no means the costs) of subscription journals—and that moving to OA should free up money that libraries could use for other purposes.

So far, that doesn't seem to be happening, and some OA advocates propose solutions that would assure it never happens, such as taking all the money now being spent on subscriptions and applying it to author-side fees and subsidies for OA journals. I suspect some of the very high author-side fees, particularly those in hybrid journals, come about not because they're justified by costs but because publishers believe they can make the case for direct substitution.

The subscription system has been broken for some time. The breakage keeps getting worse. We're long past the point where *any* institution could provide access to all the scholarly literature its researchers and other community members might be able to use, and most institutions are past the point where the damage to access is trivial. We need solutions that free up some library funding, not just transfer money from one side to another.

When will libraries see savings? I wish I had answers.

GETTING FROM HERE TO THERE

This may be the toughest aspect of OA: defining "there" and getting from here—which might be called the 20% solution—to there.

Is "there" 100% OA? If so, don't hold your breath. Aside from repeated platitudes of inevitability, I can see no plausible set of scenarios that leads us to all scholarly journals going OA or 100% of existing and future articles being deposited to OA repositories within the lifetime of any reader.

Is "there" some point—say, 75% OA—at which Big Deals become absurd and subscription journals (where subscription charges are for refereed articles as opposed to added value) become special cases? That may be more plausible, but will still require enormous change.

Why Change?

To get from 20% to 75% requires that scholars be on board—that they be willing to change existing practices. They need to prefer OA journals for new papers when that makes sense. They need to deposit existing papers and assure that they have (and use) the rights to deposit new papers when OA journals don't make sense.

Librarians need to have scholars change, but scholars need reasons to change. That's an ongoing issue for librarians and libraries, one where you can't do it yourself but need to take part in moving things forward. Some suggestions appear in chapter 5.

How Many Keystrokes Is Too Many?

For scholars to change, the personal benefits of OA repositories must outweigh the personal costs—at least for tenured scholars, where an institutional mandate carries little (if any) force. I've seen one oft-repeated estimate that it only takes ten minutes for a scholar to deposit an article in an OAI-compliant institutional repository. Is ten minutes too much? Is that a realistic estimate under most conditions and for most scholars, particularly those who don't write an article a month or even an article a year?

How many keystrokes is too many? There's no simple answer, but it's a critical question. One partial answer may be that repository staff can handle most of the keystrokes and other work—but that requires more money for repository staff.

CONCLUSIONS

If you find this chapter discouraging, you shouldn't. I'm deliberately looking for and spelling out issues to be considered, some of them ones that haven't received much attention. All of these issues are, I believe, real and legitimate. None is a showstopper. None will cripple movement toward more open access.

Will we reach a majority position for OA within my lifetime (say, 30 years), where "majority" includes existing articles as well as new ones? I'd like to think so. Within ten years? I'd be surprised. What about 75%, a possible tipping point? I'm enough of a skeptic to regard ten years as unlikely—but within my lifetime may be plausible. Movement may be slow, but it is happening.

NOTES

1. Peter Suber, "Ten challenges for open access journals," *SPARC Open Access Newsletter* #138 (October 2, 2009).
2. Walt Crawford, "Getting past the arc of enthusiasm," *Cites & Insights* 1:5 (May 2001).
3. Walt Crawford, "Pioneer OA journals: The arc of enthusiasm, five years later" and "Pioneer OA journals: Preliminary additions from DOAJ," *Cites & Insights* 6:12 (October 2006).
4. Peter Suber, Open Access Overview, 2010, www.earlham.edu/~peters/fos/overview.htm.

OPEN ACCESS
CONTROVERSIES

What's the difference between an issue and a controversy? The issues raised in chapter 3 are situations that deserve attention and study. Topics in this chapter are more controversial, or appear to be more controversial.

That's an important distinction. This chapter concerns two very different categories:

1. **Legitimate controversies:** areas about which there are sharp differences of opinion based on real evidence (or lack thereof).
2. **Pseudo-controversies:** this much larger group could be called myths, misunderstandings and straw men. These are areas proclaimed as problems with OA that lack factual evidence—or evidence that would suggest OA has problems that aren't at least true for subscription or "toll" access.

For much more detail and quite a few more examples, read Peter Suber's "A field guide to misunderstandings about open access," a 10,000-word essay in the April 2009 *SOAN Newsletter*, and "(Mis)Leading open access myths," a 5,000-word statement from BioMed Central.[1]

LEGITIMATE CONTROVERSIES
These are some of the more interesting controversial questions for open access.

How Much Value Do Publishers Add To Scholarly Articles?
Peer review, editing and copyediting, markup, distribution, promotion: We know about those functions—and we know some of them are already either free (most peer review, most editorial supervision) or can be extremely inexpensive (electronic distribution, flow control for peer review, electronic promotion).

What else do publishers bring to the table? The simplest answer is "It depends"—different publishers in different fields add different amounts and kinds of value.

T. Scott Plutchak's "The invisible parts of publishing"[2] (T. Scott, June 12, 2008) believes publishers add more value than some of us think:

We often have a tendency to glibly think (in the world of scholarly publishing, at least) that nothing of significance happens between the completion of peer review and the appearance of the published version (whether that be in print or digital form) . . .

At the *New England Journal of Medicine* (along with most other publishers), there is an army of copy-editors and illustrators and fact-checkers who come into play after the article has been accepted, all of whose skills are needed to put that article into final form and make sure that the authors' intent is conveyed in the very best way possible. You can't do that kind of work with volunteers.

And then there's the matter of getting somebody's attention. Take any article from the latest issue of *NEJM*, *Nature*, or *JAMA*. Do you really think that if you posted it on a website and invited comments (even in some mediated way so that it approximated serious peer review), and used those comments to modify and further develop the piece, it would get anywhere near the attention that it would get from having been published in one of the high-profile journals? We have a tendency to ignore the critical importance of brand in helping people make their way through the morass of content that is available.

Does Plutchak overstate the case? *PLoS One* proposes that "what's worth reading" should not be a decision made by journal editors. *Critically valuable* can be a loaded term, one that tends to favor conservatism in research. And there's a bit of a straw man in these quotations: very few OA supporters propose that all journals in all fields can or should operate without any funding or rely entirely on volunteer labor. Copyediting, markup, and promotion all require skilled effort and can be expensive. The controversy is not whether publishers add value—it boils down to how much value, whether today's brands are the only or most appropriate ones, and how best to pay for that value.

What Should It Cost To Produce an Online Journal?

This is not the same question as "Is there enough money to make OA journals work?" Some OA advocates have suggested that all the money currently spent on subscriptions (directly and through aggregated full-text databases) should be applied to author-side fees. That would certainly be "enough money," but it would also leave libraries no better off than they are now.

It seems likely that most estimates of costs by commercial subscription-journal publishers and estimates of author-side fees that would be required have been calculated by the simple expedient of dividing current revenues by the number of articles, including all current profit and overhead in the calculations along with (in some cases) the costs of print versions.

What are the real costs?

- Authors provide the papers for free—that's the basis for essentially all scholarly journal publishing.
- Nearly all peer review is also done for free. Given that submissions are handled digitally, not by mailing manuscripts around, the costs for peer review are to find appropriate reviewers and manage the process—bandwidth costs for e-mailing manuscripts are so trivial as to not be worth calculating. There are now open-source software solutions to manage peer review, but for a journal with large numbers of manuscripts, finding reviewers and managing reviews may involve significant labor costs. Analyses of the value of free peer review range from $330 million per year for reviewers in the UK to more than $3 billion worldwide.
- Many, probably most, editors work for free, possibly with some support for administrative assistance.
- Hosting costs should be small for all but the largest journals. For most journals hosted by universities and their libraries, the costs (server space and bandwidth) should be so small that they can be absorbed by the parent institution. For as little as $120/year, you can get substantial server space and bandwidth through any number of commercial services—and disk space is getting cheaper all the time.
- Setting up and maintaining a website involves some effort, but there are open-source solutions for this; the same software used to manage peer review may also be used to set up and manage the website. Open Journal Systems is a prime example of such software. It's freely distributed by the Public Knowledge Project, and it essentially maintains an online editorial office for all aspects of journal publishing.
- Any good OA journal should make provisions for redundant archiving, to improve the chances of long-term access to the articles. That's increasingly becoming easy and relatively inexpensive. One estimate is that LOCKSS, one system of assuring long-term access to digital resources, would cost about seven cents per journal year.
- That leaves copyediting, layout (markup), and marketing or publicity. What do or should these cost? In some fields and for some journals, the answer may be "little or nothing," but that may not be the best answer. The actual effort required for fully effective copyediting and professional markup will vary widely by field and complexity of papers, but it shouldn't be ignored.

That last bullet (and some provision for hosting and redundant archiving) might justify a per-article budget in the low hundreds of dollars—less in some fields, more in a few. Are there realistic justifications for author-side fees as high as $5,000? That's a tough question, one that OA advocates are generally reluctant to raise. An answer needs to show real explanations for legitimate costs that go beyond "here's our revenue for last year and how many articles we published."

Currently, Hindawi (a publisher of many gold OA journals) charges author-side fees in the low hundreds of dollars; PLoS charges range from $1,350 to $2,900; BioMed Central charges range from $740 to $2,380—and that $5,000 figure is Nature Publishing Group's charge for the a new "hybrid" *Nature Communications*. At the other extreme, one article on the true costs of e-publishing asserts a range of $64 to $76 per article, with some controversial assumptions.[3]

Can we arrive at realistic estimates for legitimate costs, possibly based on the kind of journal? Can those estimates be stated in ways most stakeholders would accept? Now, *there's* a controversy.

Would Complete OA Save Money? Could It Cost Even More?

I'm not sure this belongs in the legitimate controversy category. It's possible to create scenarios in which full gold OA would cost more for libraries and universities than the current subscription-journal system, but it requires extreme assumptions—such as assuming that per-article charges in the $3,000 to $5,000 range are universally legitimate, that all OA journals will have such ambitious charges, and that the only source of author-side fees will be universities and libraries.

None of those assumptions bears up to even slight scrutiny. In fields where grant funding pays for most research, the cost of dissemination (that is, author-side fees) can and should be included in grant totals—and some granting agencies are already doing that. In most other fields, author-side fees are likely to be smaller or nonexistent. (Remember, most existing gold OA journals don't charge author-side fees.) Attempts to model the full scholarly communications system seem to show that full OA should yield at least a 30% savings over the current environment while yielding far better results, since all articles would be available to everybody with internet connections.

Should "Delayed OA" Be Considered Open Access— and Could It Keep Subscription Journals Going?

Many subscription journals make a few teaser articles available for free immediately and open all peer-reviewed articles for all readers after an embargo period. Some OA advocates regard these journals as legitimate OA journals, if not optimal. Others don't accept that they should be called open access at all. That's one controversy (I come down on the "delayed access is not OA" side). Another is whether delayed OA is a transitional tactic or whether it makes sense for the long run. Will (and should) libraries keep paying subscription or full-text licensing fees for journals when the articles will become available at no cost in three months, six months, a year?

Green, Gold, or Both?

Stevan Harnad, an important founding voice for OA, gives lip service to the desirability of both green OA and gold OA but consistently argues against expenditures of time or money on gold OA, saying 100% green OA, which he has called "optimal and inevitable," must and should come first. Some others argue that only gold OA does any real good—although rarely in so many words. Jan Velterop seems to make this case in most of his writing about open access. Joe Dunckley argues "Green is no goal" in a June 9, 2010, post at *Journalology* (http://journalology.blogspot.com/):

> To achieve a sufficiently large but distant win, it is worth sacrificing a much smaller but nearer win if it stands in the way or distracts and delays the larger achievement. To achieve a small but near win, it is *not* worth sacrificing a much larger but more distant win. But the difference in magnitude must be sufficiently large, and the difference in distance sufficiently small, to make delaying the gratification really pay off.

Dunckley isn't interested in access as a goal: "Access is not an interesting problem." He's much more interested in how "parasitic subscription access publishers" are "slowly killing" university libraries and the "real revolution" of open data. An extreme view? Possibly—but is it more extreme than arguing that all energy should go toward green OA?

Only gold OA assures that readers won't be guided to fee-based copies of articles rather than free copies. Only gold OA definitely saves money for libraries as compared to subscription access to the same or equivalent journals. And, of course, with more than 5,000 gold OA journals already publishing, "green only" isn't going to happen.

On the other hand, a rapid transition to 100% gold OA, or even majority status for gold OA, isn't going to happen soon. It's too disruptive to commercial and society publishers, so that substantial sums will be spent to retain the subscription model for as long as possible. As long as journal brand names count, those brand names will (in some cases) come at a price. Realistically, we need both roads for OA to make real progress.

Can First-Rate No-Fee OA Journals Survive and Thrive?

Most gold OA journals do not charge author-side fees. Is that a reasonable way to build the future?

Here's part of what Peter Suber has to say about business models for non-fee OA journals:[4]

> Some no-fee OA journals have direct or indirect subsidies from institutions like universities, laboratories, research centers, libraries, hospitals, museums, learned societies, foundations, or government agencies. Some have revenue from a separate line of non-OA publications. Some have revenue from advertising, auxiliary services, membership dues, endowments, reprints, or a print or premium edition. Some rely, more than other journals, on volunteerism . . .

> We have a lot to learn from the no-fee journals. Whatever their business models, and whatever their adequacy, they have found ways to generate revenue or subsidies that other journals (both OA and non-OA) could use or try. Exposing their models to scholarly attention and community-wide discussion might even uncover ways to refine and enhance them . . .

Suber considers where no-fee and author-side fee models might work best. For example, in fields such as medicine where most articles come from grant-funded research, author-side fees represent such a tiny portion of grant funding that they may be the reasonable way to proceed.

Consider gold OA journals in the field of library and information science, a case where very few subscription charges are outrageous. As of August 9, 2010, *DOAJ*'s author list (which includes hybrid journals) includes 111 journals. Only 14 of the 111 (13%) charge author-side fees. Of 41 journals (including hybrid journals) related to organic chemistry, however, 36 (88%) charge author-side fees. The differences? That requires investigation.

Tom Wilson has published and edited *Information Research* for many years and regards gold OA journals with author-side charges as partial open access. He's now using the term *platinum OA* for what he regards as the only true open access: journals with neither subscription costs nor author charges. "Open access—again," posted June 21, 2010, at *Information Research—ideas and debate* (http://info-research.blogspot.com/), discusses the economics of journal publishing and argues that volunteer effort can reasonably eliminate essentially all costs, as it does for *Information Research*. Does the platinum model work in all fields? Perhaps not, and it would be useful to know why and where that's so.

Are Open Access Journals as Good as Subscription Journals?

There are strong OA journals and weak subscription journals. There are strong subscription journals and weak OA journals. Anyone with an ax to grind can assemble comparative lists that will hone that blade as required.

It seems to be well established that there's no clear correlation between price and quality. One might expect that, in the long run, authors would recognize that gold OA opens their readership to the world, which might make authors more careful—but how could you produce evidence of this or its inverse?

PLoS One has been derided for its "anything goes" approach, where articles are reviewed only for scientific legitimacy, not for impact—resulting in a 70% acceptance rate. The journal is now old enough to receive an impact factor—and it's a respectable number, high enough to assert quality if the impact factor means anything useful (which it may not).

Do Institutional Mandates Result in Effective Institutional Repositories?

Will an institutional mandate, even one adopted by a faculty senate rather than administrative fiat, result in an institution's faculty and scholars depositing 100% of their published articles in the institution's repository in a timely and responsible manner?

We don't know yet—such mandates haven't been around long enough. The evidence from one early mandate is positive, with one analysis claiming nearly 100% success for new articles. But there won't be strong evidence until several large institutions study deposits and publications over several years.

There's a related question: will all scholarly institutions adopt institutional OA mandates—and should they? So far, the adoption rate is slow. *Mandate* is a term many faculty loathe, and administrative mandates seem likely to engender resistance—but a growing number of mandates come from faculty senates, offering a better chance of willing compliance.

Not that universal institutional mandates (which I regard as highly unlikely) would yield 100% green OA. There are researchers outside of academia and, indeed, researchers and scholars not affiliated with any institution. Until or unless every subject has an OAI subject repository and every institution has a robust institutional repository, some articles won't be available.

What Does It Take to Make IRs Effective and Sustainable?

This may not be a controversy so much as a serious issue, one far beyond the scope of this book and my knowledge. It depends on your success criteria, for starters. As a good starting point, read Dorothea Salo's landmark article "Innkeeper at the roach motel" in *Library Trends* 57:2 (Fall 2008), available as a green OA postprint at http://minds.wisconsin.edu/bitstream/handle/1793/22088/Salo_Final.pdf?sequence=6, particularly the section "What must happen."

What Would Happen to Subscription Journals if 100% Green OA Is Achieved?

A narrower form of that question: would 100% green OA result in serials cancellations, and to what extent? The overall questions are hugely controversial.

At one extreme, it seems unlikely that *Science* or *Nature* would lose all their subscriptions if all peer-reviewed articles were known to be available from repositories. These journals have too many noninstitutional subscribers and offer too much added value to disappear overnight.

At the other extreme, I would be astonished to see any library retain a subscription to LIS journals costing $2,000 to $10,000 and up if the articles were known to be available through green OA, if those subscriptions aren't hidden within bundles sold at heavy discounts from fantasy list prices.

There is no question that some journals can retain reasonably priced subscriptions while going to gold OA, either for added value or for print copies. If gold OA journals can do so, it seems likely that journals made partially redundant through green OA could also do so—but not at the high prices currently being charged in some cases.

Finally, here's one that's a real controversy not directly related to any specific aspect of open access:

Do the Tone and Content of Some OA Advocacy Distract from Improving Access to Scholarship?

T. Scott Plutchak thinks they do—to the extent that he's said he's disgusted with the open access movement. I think repeated, strident calls to focus all attention on one aspect of OA and personal attacks on those who feel differently have the net result of alienating people who would otherwise support forward movement. Similarly, assertions that OA repositories are essentially free make life difficult for people trying to develop and run effective institutional repositories that cost real money.

It cuts both ways, to be sure. Some of those who oppose OA—especially those who implicitly oppose it or work to undermine it—use fallacies, personal attacks, and misleading assumptions to slow the progress of OA. Some who appear to support gold

OA do so in a manner that works to undermine all OA, by supporting only forms of OA that would keep publishers and their profits whole. Misleading tone and content are always with us.

MYTHS AND MISUNDERSTANDINGS

Any number of publishers, including commercial publishers and society publishers earning surpluses from journal subscriptions, has offered these myths as reasons to oppose open access. Two organizations (or, in one case, pseudo-organization) seem to exist largely to maintain these pseudo-controversies. Most notoriously, PRISM, the so-called Partnership for Research Integrity in Science & Medicine, was created by the Professional & Scholarly Publishing Division of the Association of American Publishers to fight against "government mandates"—the NIH mandate and proposed acts to improve public access to publicly funded research such as FRPAA, the Federal Research Public Access Act. The website is still there with no updates since 2007. The other, the DC Principles Coalition, claims to support "broad access to the scientific and medical literature"—but in a manner that's very different from open access and works to undermine open access. The group has consistently worked to reverse the NIH mandate and expansion of public access to publicly funded research, propounding the myth that open access undermines copyright. The coordinator of the DC Principles Coalition, Martin Frank of the American Physiological Society, is one of the most active proponents of anti-OA myths.

Subheadings here are statements rather than questions. In every case, the statement is either false or exaggerated, or applies at least as much to subscription journals as it does to OA journals. For those statements related to green OA, the statements are either false or exaggerated. Some of these are misunderstandings rather than deliberate myths—not so much attempts to undermine open access as simple failures to understand it fully. This is, to be sure, an incomplete list.

OA Undermines Peer Review

Simply not true. Both gold OA and green OA *presume* proper peer review, using exactly the same methodology as in peer-reviewed subscription journals.

There are people who feel that traditional peer review no longer works—but such feelings are not part of any OA movement.

Publishers repeat this myth despite a complete lack of evidence. When FRPAA (which would mandate open access to government-funded research) was first proposed, the AAP claimed that it "could well have the unintended consequence of compromising or destroying the independent system of peer review that ensures the integrity of the very research the U.S. Government is trying to support and disseminate." The DC Principles Coalition claimed that FRPAA would result in a rapid decline in journals that consist largely of federally funded research and that "subscription revenues support the quality control system known as peer review." Similarly, the Association of Learned and Professional Society Publishers (ALPSP) and International Association of Scientific, Technical & Medical Publishers (IASTM), opposing a proposed open access mandate for the European Union, asserted, "Open deposit of accepted manuscripts risks destabilising subscription revenues and undermining peer review." PRISM went further, claiming that OA policies would "jeopardize the financial viability of the journals that conduct peer review, placing the entire scholarly communication process at risk."[5]

Saying a thing three times does not make it true, despite Lewis Carroll's poetry—and saying a thing hundreds of times, or specifically linking subscription revenues to peer review, does not make this nonsense believable. Not that this deters opponents of OA: an April 29, 2010, letter from some members of AAP's Professional and Scholarly Publishing Committee to Congress, opposing FRPAA (still on the legislative agenda), claims once again that it "would undermine copyright and adversely impact the existing peer review system."

There are OA journals that use editorial quality control rather than full peer review, just as there are subscription journals that do exactly the same thing. Most OA journals use traditional peer review and, as with subscription journals, nearly all peer review is done for free by other researchers and scholars, not paid out of subscription revenues.

There's a related myth, and this one's a little more complicated:

Gold OA Publishing with Author-Side Fees Weakens Peer Review

The claim is that, since author-side fees are almost universally charged only for accepted articles, OA publishers will be tempted to accept marginal papers in order to increase revenues.

This myth has been stated in a different manner: open access threatens scientific integrity due to a conflict of interest resulting from charging authors. Here's a terse response to this myth from "(Mis)Leading open access myths"[6]

> The assertion being made is, essentially, that Open Access publishers have an incentive to publish dubious material, in order to increase their revenue from Article Processing Charges. This is a very peculiar accusation for [traditional publishers] to make given that [their subscription price increases are primarily justified on the basis that they are publishing more articles]. In which case, if their own argument is to be believed, they face the exactly the same conflict of interest as Open Access publishers.

> Fortunately, however, no such conflict of interest exists, for either Open Access or traditional publishers. Any scientific journal's success depends on authors choosing to submit their research to it for publication. Authors publish research in order for the value of their findings to be recognized . . . If a journal had a reputation for publishing poor science, it would not receive submissions . . .

Consider these facts:

- Many subscription publishers justify price increases based on increased numbers of published articles. They have a direct incentive to accept more papers.

- Not only do many more subscription journals than OA journals charge author-side fees, a higher percentage of subscription journals charge author-side fees for accepted articles. Thus, if there's any temptation for OA journals to accept marginal papers, the temptation is greater for subscription journals.
- Most gold OA publishers have careful, explicit procedures in place to maintain a firewall between financial and editorial matters, just as ethical subscription publishers have such firewalls. Since most gold OA journals that do charge author-side fees also have waiver procedures for those unable to pay (or for other reasons), reviewers don't know whether a proposed paper will come with a fee.
- The second quoted paragraph is controlling: journals survive only if they get submissions, and authors don't submit papers to journals with reputations for accepting shoddy scholarship.

Green OA frequently means depositing versions of papers that have not yet been peer-reviewed—but they should be marked as such, and authors (and repository managers) have strong incentives to be sure that papers are identified as peer reviewed and published once that's the case.

Author-Side Fees Come Out of the Author's Pocket

That's not impossible but it's unlikely in most cases—which is why I use *author-side* rather than *author* and why *processing fees* may be better than *author-side fees*. There's a related misunderstanding, namely that author-side fees mean well-funded researchers have more access to publication outlets than poorly funded ones do.

- A growing number of research grants include provisions for payment of author-side fees. For STEM, the highest author-side fees represent such a tiny percentage of total research costs that this is an entirely reasonable inclusion.
- Of the minority of gold OA journals that charge author-side fees, most (if not all) provide fee waivers for authors unable to pay—and, in some cases, the waiver does not require explanation.
- A small but growing number of institutions have OA funds to pay author-side fees when grant funds don't already provide for such fees. Current experience suggests that such funds don't cost much on a per-capita basis because there aren't many cases where they're needed, and they eliminate inability to pay as an argument against OA— within those institutions.

Author-Side Fees Prevent Scholars in Developing Nations from Publishing

OA, whether gold or green, improves the ability of researches in developing nations because it assures that they can read existing papers. In practice, most gold OA journals with author-side fees provide broad waivers for developing nations, so this isn't an issue in any case. Developing nations are also founding their own journals, mostly online and OA, a heartening development for scholarship and global diversity.

OA Advocates Claim that Online Publishing Doesn't Cost Any Money

No serious open access advocate has ever said that online publishing, whether open access or not, was without cost—although some have said (correctly) that for some smaller journals the costs are so low that they can be covered by trivial departmental subsidies. It seems likely that online publishing costs can be dramatically lower than existing publishing systems, but there are always costs.

As Peter Suber said when responding to this claim being promulgated by a professional society publisher in 2005: "To say so at this late date, after this old misinformation has repeatedly been corrected, is to show that one is not paying attention."

Open Access Is Only about Publishing

By now, you know the answer to this: green OA, depositing peer-reviewed papers in subject or institutional repositories, is an equally valid form of open access. Of course, there's also the opposite assertion, which is more of a controversy than a misunderstanding:

The Costs of Open Access Will Reduce Funding for Research

One analysis of biomedical research (one of the most expensive research areas) suggests that the total amount of money that goes to support traditional publishing, including very high profit margins for the largest commercial publishers and the added costs of print distribution and inefficient production systems, amounts to no more than 1% to 2% of the funds devoted to biomedical research. That's a worst-case scenario. In most fields, open access costs should amount to little more than a rounding error in research funding.

Arguments against the NIH mandate to deposit articles resulting from NIH-funded research into PubMed Central have included claims that maintaining an enlarged PubMed Central would significantly shrink funds available for research support. NIH has said that full compliance with the mandate could result in an annual cost of $15 million to operate PubMed Central. That may seem like a lot, but that's out of a $28 billion NIH research budget. In other words, the cost of green OA for these articles comes out to just over one-twentieth of 1% of the research funding or $1 out of every $2,000.

Researchers Already Have All the Access They Need

A narrower version of this argument is a claim that researchers at institutions of higher education in the United Kingdom have access to 97% of journals in ScienceDirect. Similarly, it's assumed that most researchers in the U.S. are at very large universities that have Big Deals providing access to nearly all scientific journals. For example, in a 2010 hearing on FRPAA, Alan Adler claimed that "there is no crisis in the world of scholarly publishing, or in the dissemination of scientific materials."

This argument fails the sniff test. Even researchers at the largest universities don't have access to all the journals they could use, particularly as growing costs require cancellations. This says nothing about researchers at smaller institutions and outside academia, and the hapless situation of independent scholars, practitioners, and lay readers.

The situation is far worse in most countries. There are programs by which some journals are available for free in some developing nations—but, for example, the HINARI and AGORA initiatives provide about 2,000 journals for free only to the poorest countries and with very limited access in those countries. Countries such as India, Pakistan, and Indonesia are not part of the deals; neither are Brazil and China. Researchers in these nations, and researchers at all but the wealthiest institutions in first-world nations, do not have ready access to all the research in their field.

The Public Can Always Get Access to Articles from Their Public Libraries

Realistically, and even assuming everyone has access to public libraries (not true in the U.S., much less most less-developed nations), this only works via interlibrary loan, since few public libraries can afford (or would spend their funds on) Big Deals.

"(Mis)Leading open access myths" puts it this way:

> To say that being able to go to the library and request an interlibrary loan is a substitute for having Open Access to research articles online is rather like saying that carrier pigeon is a substitute for the Internet.

> Yes—both can convey information, but attempting to watch a live video stream with data delivered by carrier pigeon would be a frustrating business. Practically, the obstacles to obtaining an article via the interlibrary loan route are so huge that all but the most determined members of the public are put off . . .

This also assumes that online or print journal subscriptions allow for unlimited provision of ILL copies of articles, decidedly not the case. This assertion might better be stated: "Determined members of the public who have access to the wealthiest public libraries *may* be able to obtain articles in some cases if they're patient enough."

Scholarly Articles Are Intended for Other Scholars and Would Just Confuse Laymen

This one's been stated differently for medical research: patients would be confused by access to peer-reviewed medical literature, and doctors don't want their patients to be confused.

There are doubtless some doctors who would just as soon that their patients not be more up-to-date on a particular medical situation than the doctors are. More enlightened doctors are only too happy to have patients directly involved in awareness and care, and many laypeople are quite capable of understanding scholarly research. This is a particularly obnoxious elitist argument.

Publishers Need to Acquire Copyright to Protect the Integrity of Scholarly Articles

Here's an odd one: claims by publishers that copyright transfer, which can get in the way of green OA, is needed so they can protect authors from plagiarism or outright theft. That's nonsense; there are few if any cases where copyright law has been used to defend the integrity of a scientific paper. BioMed Central has said it "knows of no situation where this has happened." In practice, effective OA discourages plagiarism and theft by making it easier to identify the original of a paper.

Open Access Eliminates (or Weakens or Violates) Copyright

Quite the opposite, from an author's perspective. Gold OA journals typically leave copyright in the name of the authors—and if not, such journals would retain copyright.

Providing free access is not the same as abandoning copyright. The most straightforward way for OA journals to handle this is to adopt a Creative Commons license (ideally attribution or BY, alternatively attribution-noncommercial or BY-NC), which explicitly grants needed rights while retaining copyright.

Green open access at the preprint stage does not violate copyright: at that point, the author holds copyright. You hold copyright in your work as soon as it's created— effectively, as soon as you save it to disk or other stable memory. The only way you can give up copyright is through a formal assignment, and submitting a manuscript does not constitute such an assignment. Neither does its acceptance: only a separate signed agreement can turn over copyright.

Does OA weaken copyright? Not if you believe in the constitutional basis of copyright, "to promote the progress of science and useful arts." OA strengthens that aspect of copyright, as it makes work more readily available to those who could take progress further. If you believe that copyright's purpose is to yield the maximum possible revenue for the copyright holder, then you could make this claim—but scholarly articles typically return zero revenue to authors, so it's a meaningless claim.

Open Access Destroys Incentive

There are two versions of this one: open access deprives authors of royalties, or open access destroys the incentive to create good work.

The first one is a myth for the obvious reason that contemporary open access is about work that does not generate royalties for authors. Few advocates of open access argue that people should make their books available for free; there are arguments for such experiments, but they're not part of the open access movement as such.

The second gets it exactly wrong. One incentive to write good scholarly articles should be to have people read them and make effective use of your research. By making it possible for *everybody* to read your articles, you enhance that incentive.

Most Scholars Don't Self-Archive, so They Must Be Opposed to Open Access

The first part of this assertion is true. At best, self-archiving seems to cover 15% to 20% of new research articles. It's not possible to disprove the second part of this assertion in general—but it is noteworthy that, for the past two or three years, most new OA mandates have been adopted by faculty vote rather than administrative fiat. When asked (with enough information), most faculty members are willing to comply with mandates—and when faculty senates unanimously adopt mandates, it's fair to assume they're not opposed to their effects.

There are two obvious reasons for low rates of self-archiving:

Ignorance: Most faculty members and other researchers are too busy with teaching and research to spend much time learning about open access.

Inertia: Until faculty members and other scholars understand the direct and indirect benefits of OA, it's easiest to keep on doing what they've been doing.

It's Free: What More Do You Want?

This isn't a myth and not a complete misunderstanding. It is, instead, a limiting simplification—it equates gratis OA with all OA.

Removing price barriers is great, but removing permission barriers can lead to important new scholarship. Libre open access (discussed in chapter 2) has clear advantages over gratis OA. Unfortunately, a fair number of OA journals don't get this—too many of them don't have clear licenses permitting more than just reading.

And Ever So Many More . . .

I'm not discussing other myths and misunderstandings. You'll find some of them in the sources listed in the endnotes.

NOTES

1. Peter Suber, "A field guide to misunderstandings about open access," *SPARC Open Access Newsletter* #132 (April 2, 2009); Open Access Now, (Mis)Leading open access myths, www.biomedcentral.com/openaccess/inquiry/myths/?myth=all.

2. T. Scott Plutchak, The invisible parts of publishing, 2008, http://tscott.typepad.com/tsp/2008/06/the-invisible-p.html.

3. Julian H. Fisher, "Scholarly publishing re-invented: real costs and real freedoms," *The Journal of Electronic Publishing* 21:2 (Spring 2008).

4. Peter Suber, "No-fee open-access journals," *SPARC Open Access Newsletter* #103, (November 2, 2006).

5. Quotations from Peter Suber, "Will open access undermine peer review?" *SPARC Open Access Newsletter* #113, (September 2, 2007).

6. Open Access Now, "Myths."

5

TAKING
ACTION

What should you and your library be doing about open access?
Some of the suggestions that follow are primarily for academic librarians, special librarians (in institutions with research components), and public librarians in public libraries that are also research libraries. The first five apply to all librarians and libraries. Library schools need to deal with all of these, especially the last one.

Even more than the rest of this book, this chapter offers starting points. Whether you're working with researchers, considering an institutional repository, or building an OA publishing operation, you'll need a lot more information than this book provides.

THE FIVE BASICS

Every library person should think about these five areas, at least enough to see whether they apply in your case.

1. Understanding the Situation

You've been exposed to some of the reasons open access matters for your users and your library. You know the basics of open access. You're aware of some real issues and some of the pervasive myths surrounding OA.

If you don't believe the current system is broken, you need to. As Dorothea Salo put it in a May 4, 2010, posting at *The Book of Trogool* after returning from a UKSG conference on serials issues, "No more can-kicking." That is: "We can't keep kicking the journal-cost can down the street any longer. Serials expenditures cannot and will not continue at their current level, much less increase." Salo says publishers are beginning to recognize this—and so must all librarians. Without open access, availability of the research literature will continue to shrink.

Thinking about your library's role may require some rethinking. If you believe your mission is to buy appropriate materials for your patrons, spending on behalf of OA may seem outside the mission. If you believe your mission is to *make appropriate materials available*, spending on behalf of OA is a necessary part of a virtuous circle that will improve access at all institutions, yours included. (Thanks to Dorothea Salo for raising this issue and Barbara Fister for commenting on it in "Open access and the library's missing mission," published August 18, 2010, at *Library Babel Fish*, www.insidehighered .com/blogs/library_babel_fish.)

You need to be aware of the complexities of open access and the extent to which it's a moving target. A few examples:

- Open access is a goal. It is not a business model. At present, at least, green OA doesn't inherently affect or compromise subscription journals . . . but at some point, it seems likely to do so. Similarly, gold OA—journals that don't charge for access to peer-reviewed articles—is neither a business model nor a monolithic author-side fees proposition. There are many different ways for gold OA journals to be funded and to succeed.

- It's possible and likely that open access will succeed in part but not reach 100% of the literature. There's no question that OA journals can coexist with subscription journals. There's almost no question that some subscription journals will still be around in a decade and probably in several decades. By some standards, the current 20% estimate (20% of journals being OA and, independently, 20% of articles being OA through green or gold means) is an enormous success for a young endeavor. Not reaching 100% will not be failure and is no reason for despair—it can still help to get from 20% to, say, 50% or 75%.

- Different fields have different needs, and it's likely that we'll see different approaches to OA and much different rates of adoption in different communities. The high-energy physics community has adopted a subject-archive approach, arXiv, that's been enormously successful—but many other disciplines seem more likely to rely on institutional archives. The issue of affordability for author-side processing fees is very different for science, technology, and medicine, where nearly all research is funded by healthy grants than it is for humanities areas with little or no grant funding and a good deal of unfunded research. $1,350 is almost trivial for a grant-funded biomedical researcher. $1,350 for me, as an independent library researcher with no institutional affiliation, would be prohibitive.

- OA is a moving target. Five years ago most observers would have considered deposit of an article PDF in a repository to be fully acceptable green OA—and, in some humanities fields, that's probably true today. Now, with more emphasis on reusability of research, many observers would consider PDF deposits seriously compromised, and some don't call them OA. Similarly, business models for OA journals and ways to make institutional repositories work are constantly changing as we learn more and see problems.

2. Communicating with Your Community

Whether you're at a major university or a small-town library, there are people within your community who will benefit from open access. You should help get the word out. Find ways to communicate the advantages of open access for patients, people who want to understand topics deeply, journalists, and others. People need to know *how* to find open access articles, *why* they should care about them, *where* to look further before paying for a copy of an article (or giving up on the article) and *what* to do to encourage more open access, including full OA for federally funded research through FRPAA. You're a librarian; you know (or should know) the tools and how to use them effectively.

3. Encouraging Equal (or Better) Findability

Even the smallest and most badly funded library should have free access to 20% of current scientific literature, as long as you have Internet access. But are OA journals and articles in OA repositories findable within your library? Are they at least as findable as articles in subscription journals?

There are two parts to that question, both of which may take some research on your part:

- Do you provide, highlight, and understand the free indexes for OA literature, including OAIster, web search engines, and others?
- Do the indexing services you offer provide equal support for OA journals within their fields? If not, can you help convince them to do so? Are there mechanisms to get from retrieved citations within subscription journals to OA copies of those articles when you don't already have access to the full-text journals?

4. Thinking about Your Own Writing and Open Access

Do you write scholarly articles within library and information science or in any other field? Do you plan to do so?

If so, have you considered open access?

While there are more than 100 gold OA journals within library and information science, relatively few of the best-known names offer gold OA—but many support green OA and a growing number provide delayed access to articles.

Your considerations here might be the same as for any scholar:

- First, check the gold OA journals within the field where your article belongs. Is one of those a suitable outlet? If so, submit your article there first—and, if you have acquaintances on the editorial boards of subscription journals, explain why you're doing that.
- Second, if you're working with a subscription journal, examine the author agreement carefully. Some journals now have clean green OA agreements, explicitly permitting immediate deposit of the article in its final form. Others have more than one agreement—one transferring copyright and not explicitly dealing with green OA, one not transferring copyright and granting certain rights to the publisher in a manner that protects green OA. Use the latter.
- If you don't find a suitable agreement, consider an author addendum to the existing agreement. The addendum modifies the publisher's contract to retain some rights that the default contract would give to the publisher. "Navigating Publisher Agreements" at Academic

Commons, Columbia's repository, provides a good summary on retaining author rights. You'll find it at http://cdrs.columbia.edu/academiccommons/?p=259.

- If none of this works, talk to the journal editor about OA issues and why you believe your article (and all articles) should be freely available.
- Times change. When you have another article ready, see how the landscape has changed. Journals may have shortened embargoes or gone fully OA, or new OA journals may exist that would make great homes for your articles.

There's another piece for some of you. If you serve on an editorial board or as an editor, how does your journal deal with access? If it's not gold OA, can it at least be fully green OA—and, preferably, have the shortest possible embargo for free online access to published articles? Access six months after publication isn't ideal, but it's better than nothing.

5. Keeping Up to Date

If this publication had appeared in 2007, it would not have mentioned *gratis* and *libre*, since those terms hadn't been used for open access. At this point, they're tricky terms: *libre* covers too much ground to suit advocates of true open science, for example.

Things change. New OA journals appear—some of them, sad to say, largely scams, but many of them new challenges to existing journals. Some journals convert to OA and others try hybrid models. More institutions adopt OA mandates or resolutions.

Things change. The broken model of traditional subscription journals is getting more broken all the time. Unfortunately, there's reason to believe that it isn't the big commercial publishers and overpriced journals that will be hit first as the subscription model continues to crumble. The first to go may be journals with smaller audiences and lesser reputations, including many of the more reasonably priced journals and those in the humanities.

Chapter 6 offers a few resources available for you to keep up to date. You can't individually follow them all, at least not unless that's your full-time job description. You can follow some of them—and all but the smallest academic libraries should be able to see that most, if not all, are followed often enough to stay current.

WORKING WITH SCHOLARS AND RESEARCHERS

You can't do it alone. In the real world, establishing an OA repository and achieving a mandate to use that repository may not do much. You need your community's scholars and researchers to understand open access, support open access and, perhaps most difficult to achieve, act on that support. If the faculty at an institution agree that all articles should be OA, there's a much better chance that scholars will take the time to make it happen.

The next six subheadings are issues raised by Peter Suber in "Six things researchers need to know about open access," the lead essay in *SPARC Open Access Newsletter* #94

(February 2, 2006). The comments on those questions are partly Suber's, partly mine. The seventh subheading is an issue I believe to be equally relevant, while the eighth may only be relevant to some researchers. These are things every scholar needs to know—and they're areas where librarians can and should help scholars and researchers.

1. What OA journals exist in your field? Why don't scholars publish in OA journals? One frequent reason, according to some research, is that they don't know enough about OA journals in their field.

You can help. Go to the *DOAJ*. Find the disciplines that are most appropriate for your scholars, and go over the list with them. Maybe they'll find a suitable outlet. Maybe they won't.

This isn't a one-time process. Make sure your scholars know about *DOAJ* and recheck it when they're writing new papers. Next year—*next month*—things may have changed.

2. OA journals are not the whole story of OA. There are also OA archives or repositories. If your scholars don't find OA journals suitable, they should consider OA repositories.

Does your campus have an institutional repository? If so, encourage your community members to use it—and explain the issues of clearing rights and author addenda. If not, should you? For that matter, is there an appropriate subject repository?

Many institutional repositories and some subject repositories will have much that is *not* peer-reviewed literature, and OA repositories don't perform peer review. But articles within those repositories should be clearly identified as to whether they've passed peer review and where they've been published. For an institutional repository, the "other stuff" may be a good reason for your scholars to get involved—they may find that a well-managed institutional repository becomes a valuable tool throughout their research process.

Two good places to look for OA repositories: the Registry of Open Access Repositories (ROAR), at http://roar.eprints.org/, including 1,869 repositories in late September 2010, and OpenDOAR (Directory of Open Access Repositories), at www.opendoar.org, an "authoritative directory of academic open access repositories" that have been "visited by project staff" and has 1,731 listings in late September 2010. As of this writing, OpenDOAR includes a search capability for content within the repositories—one that does not rely on the OAI-PMH protocol. The same appears to be true for ROAR; both systems use Google Custom Search as a search engine.

3. OA archiving takes only a few minutes. According to one study of log activity at a heavily used institutional repository, it took an average of ten minutes to deposit a paper. If your library actively supports or maintains an institutional repository, you may have ways to cut this minimal effort even further or shift it from scholars to other staff. You can also help scholars make most efficient use of your repository or any other repository they use.

4. Most non-OA journals allow authors to deposit their postprints in an OA repository. The best current estimate is that 70% of non-OA journals consent in advance to postprint archiving and as many as 93% allow preprint archiving. A relatively small (and shrinking) percentage of journals does not allow for any form of green OA. Every scholar should be prepared to ask, "Why not?" if publishing with one of the remaining holdouts.

5. Journals using the Ingelfinger rule are a shrinking minority. This is "inside baseball," but deals with the fear of some authors that they won't be able to get an article published if they've deposited a preliminary version in an OA repository. The "Ingelfinger rule," named after a former editor at the *New England Journal of Medicine*, forbade publication of any paper that had previously circulated as preprints or where results had been publicized.

The rule is extremely rare outside of medicine and is getting less common even within that field. Still, you should help scholars understand the possibility and how to avoid problems.

6. OA enlarges your audience and citation impact. This is the chief reason for authors to provide OA to their own work. OA increases the audience for a work far beyond the audience of any subscription journal, even the most prestigious or popular journal. Studies in many fields show a correlation between OA and citation-count increases from 50% to 250%.

Providing OA to your own work is not an act of charity that only benefits others or a sacrifice justified only by the greater good. It's not a sacrifice at all. It increases your visibility, retrievability, audience, usage, and citations. It's about career-building. For publishing scholars, it would be a bargain even if it were costly, difficult, and time consuming.

The Spread of OA Can Improve Your Own Research

You and your researchers don't have ready access to all the research results that could assist them in their own research. Even the wealthiest university libraries can no longer afford every journal that might be useful. That's the flipside of making your articles available to everyone else: the more people who use OA techniques, the more articles you'll be able to read when you need them. That's a straightforward benefit in time, money, and avoiding redundant effort.

OA Is Not "Open Science"—But It's a Necessary Component

Open access is just one of the Opens you may hear about these days. Two others—open data, the concept that data sets should be openly available for other researchers to take advantage, and open notebooks, the concept that scientists should make their working notes openly available—are becoming popular. The combination of these three and, possibly, other Opens can be enlarged into open science.

Open access is not enough for open science, but you can't have open science without open access: it's necessary but not sufficient. Open access isn't all about science, of course; the humanities can also gain through OA.

INSTITUTIONAL REPOSITORIES

Does your institution already have an OAI-compliant institutional repository?

Check ROAR and OpenDOAR. Checked in late September 2010, ROAR lists 339 OA repositories in the U.S. and 59 in Canada; OpenDOAR lists 373 in the U.S. and 54 in Canada. Examples of Canadian academic institutional repositories include T-Space at the University of Toronto (20,903 records when last examined by ROAR), eScholarship@McGill at McGill University (20,781), and UWSpace at the University of Waterloo (3,534). U.S. academic institutional repositories include ScholarsArchive at Brigham Young University (355,291 records at last check), Deep Blue at the University of Michigan (59,861), the original DSpace at MIT (42,955), and DASH Digital Access to Scholarship at Harvard (3,290—but it's only been active for a year or so).

If your institution already has a repository, should the library be working to make it more effective? If it doesn't, should the library establish one?

Open Access Mandates

Should your institution mandate OA—that is, insist that all scholarly articles by researchers within the institution either appear in gold OA journals or be deposited in institutional or subject repositories? That's not an easy question. More to the point, a mandate doesn't assure compliance, and a mandate for future articles does little or nothing to increase the availability of existing articles.

If your campus doesn't have an OA mandate (or has one that isn't working), you should read "Opening the door: How faculty authors can implement an open access policy at their institutions" by Simon J. Frankel and Shannon M. Nestor of Covington & Burling LLP, prepared as a white paper on behalf of SPARC and the Science Commons. You'll find it—in open access PDF form—at http://sciencecommons.org/wp-content/uploads/Opening-the-Door.pdf.

OA PUBLISHING

Should your library—particularly if you're in an academic library—provide publishing support for new OA journals?

That's an easy question with difficult answers. You may find that your campus already has a growing OA presence—one that the library could enhance or work with. You may find that your university press or journal publishers on campus need help in forming effective OA methodologies, and you can provide that help and coordination.

There's a lot to explore—open journal systems and other open-source systems for managing OA journals, just as a starter. It may be a worthwhile exploration. Don't expect overnight results and don't be discouraged if a journal fails to achieve overnight success. *The Public-Access Computer Systems Review*, the pioneer OA journal in library and information science, faded away after seven strong years but produced articles of lasting significance (not all peer-reviewed) during its life. *Information Research* is now in its 15th year as an OA journal, with a strong record of significant articles—produced with neither subscription charges nor author-side fees.

Open Access Funds

There's another way institutions can subsidize open access publishing: institutional funds to pay author-side fees. A few universities already have such funds, and Charles D. Eckman and Beth T. Wolf (University of California, Berkeley) argue that the time is right in "Institutional open access funds: Now is the time," a perspective in *PLoS Biology* (www.plosbiology.org/article/info%3Adoi%2F10.1371%2Fjournal.pbio.1000375). It's an interesting argument, but raises a question: are the author-side fees supported by such funds *reasonable* fees? Is this an efficient use of universities' limited funds? Read the article—which appears in an OA journal with high author-side fees. You'll find a list of institutions with journal funds at http://oad.simmons.edu/oadwiki/OA_journal_funds; as of September 6, 2010, the page shows more than two dozen funds, but at least one of them has already shut down.

Stuart Shieber argues that the right kind of open access fund costs "almost nothing" in "How much does a COPE-compliant open-access fund cost?" posted August 6, 2010, at *The Occasional Pamphlet* (http://blogs.law.harvard.edu/pamphlet/). The "right kind" of fund only supports author-side fees for full gold OA journals (no fees for hybrid journals) and only supports such fees when the research in question was not grant-funded. Given those limits and Shieber's version of "almost nothing," he's right—but that can still mean thousands or tens of thousands of dollars per year. The study shows that most of the funds studied really didn't pay for much of anything, with only four funds paying for more than three articles per year.

CONTRIBUTING TO RESEARCH

You might consider taking a different kind of active role: research some of the issues around open access and ancillary areas.

There are many open research questions, areas either where there's not yet enough data to draw conclusions or where nobody's done the hard work to pull that data together. In some cases, there has been research, but it's been done with such flawed assumptions and inherent bias that it's hard to credit the results. Even where research has been done, much of it requires longitudinal work, repeated in a consistent manner over a period of time in order to demonstrate trends.

A few examples of open research questions, excerpted and sometimes reworded from a much longer list from the *Open Access Directory* at http://oad.simmons.edu/oadwiki/Research_questions:

- What is the current rate of self-archiving in different fields and countries? Can we graph the change in these rates over time? Can we disentangle spontaneous self-archiving from self-archiving encouraged or required by funders and universities? Can we calculate both the percentage of self-archiving authors and the percentage of self-archived papers?
- You can't answer the questions in the previous or following bullet without answering another underlying question: how much publishing is there in a particular discipline? Are there reasonably

reliable ways of estimating the annual and total number of articles published within a discipline?

- What percentage of published articles from a given year or a given journal has OA copies somewhere online? Can we break this down by permitted copies and unpermitted ones? Can we break it down by preprints and postprints? Can we break it down by field? Can we collect these numbers easily enough to recompute them annually and chart future progress?

- When a subscription-access (or "toll access") journal converts to open access, does its impact factor go up, remain the same, or decline?

- What percentage of peer-reviewed, free online journals goes beyond removing price barriers to the removal of at least some permission barriers? Of those removing permission barriers, how many use a CC-BY license (or equivalent), a CC-BY-NC license (or equivalent), and so on?

- Only a minority of OA journals charge author-side publication fees. What are the other OA journal business models? The first phase of this research is simply to document the range of models actually in use. The second phase is to study which models work best, and worst, in which niches.

- Are researchers responding to funder and university open access policies by changing the patterns of where they submit their work for publication?

- When researchers learn about a subscription-journal article of interest to them, how often do they look online for an OA copy? When they do so, where do they look?

- How much time does it take for a university to create and maintain an OAI-compliant OA repository? How much does it cost the university, in hardware, software, and human resources? If it depends on how much the university wants to do with the repository, and how much to educate users, then can we break down the costs for each layer of use and service?

If that seems like a long list of questions, go to the OAD page—the full list is much longer. Some of these may be questions where you and your institution could take the lead. Some, perhaps most, will require a form of crowdsourcing, distributing research questions among many institutions. Many of these questions fall solidly within the field of library and information science, and the better journals in the field should be only too happy to publish the results.

CONCLUSION

We're not there yet. Chances are, we won't be for quite a while—and if "there" means 100% availability of all past, present, and future research articles, it's quite possible that we'll never be there.

But more of the literature is freely available now than a year ago, and it seems likely that a higher percentage of peer-reviewed articles will be available through OA methods next year than are available now. Beyond articles, there is and will be growing open access to media resources and datasets.

We're likely to see tipping points. When more than half of current peer-reviewed articles are openly available and when article-level metrics demonstrate convincingly that open access makes articles not only more widely read but more widely used, we'll start to see major changes for the good. When two-thirds of all peer-reviewed articles are openly available, OA will be the norm—not universal, but assuring effective, immediate access to most literature. Those are ambitious goals, but they're not impossible. Librarians can help get us there.

Charles W. Bailey Jr. offers another set of possible actions for libraries and librarians in the "The role of libraries in open access" section of "Open access and libraries," *Collection Management* 32:3/4 (2007), www.digital-scholarship.org/cwb/OALibraries2.pdf.

OA can be a frustrating field to follow, particularly given the repeated untruths from some sectors and the repeated arguments within the field. But it's also an exciting field, one where we *are* seeing progress in an area all librarians should applaud: toward making more knowledge available to more people regardless of their economic or geographic situation.

6

EXPLORING
OPEN ACCESS

Y ou need to keep up with developments in open access, not only to help move it forward but also to assure that your library and patrons can make the most of what's available. This book offers a quick introduction, but the literature of open access is rich and complex—and mostly available for free. This chapter doesn't attempt completeness. It's not a bibliography or webliography, although it includes pointers to one or two of them. It's an annotated set of items I believe will help you explore open access now and in the future.

KEY SOURCES

These are the cornerstones: the resources you should check first. One or two of these may be a bit overwhelming, but if you can follow all of these, you'll be extremely well informed about open access.

SPARC Open Access Newsletter. Peter Suber began writing the *Free Online Scholarship (FOS) Newsletter* (ISSN 1535-7848) in March 2001, continuing through September 2002 for a total of 62 issues. With the support of the Scholarly Publishing & Academic Resources Coalition (SPARC), Suber restarted the newsletter in a new monthly form in July 2003 as the *SPARC Open Access Newsletter* (ISSN 1546-7821), numbering issues beginning with #63 for continuity. *SOAN* has appeared regularly ever since, almost always on the second day of each month. *SOAN* is distributed by e-mail subscription; to subscribe, send any message to SPARC-OANews-feed@arl.org. A complete searchable archive is at www.earlham.edu/~peters/fos/newsletter/archive.htm. The SPARC page for subscriptions to *SOAN* (and the SPARC Open Access Forum) is at www.arl.org/sparc/publications/soan/.

SOAN is *the* key monthly publication on open access. Issues typically begin with a major essay and continue with a set of annotated links to "what happened, or what I noticed, since the last issue of the newsletter, emphasizing action and policy over scholarship and opinion." Coming events and housekeeping items round out each issue.

Typical issues of *SOAN* are shorter than 25 printable pages. Lead essays provide practical and philosophical understanding of open access issues. Suber believes wholeheartedly in the worth of open access but is not afraid to address problems. He is a fair, honest, and excellent writer.

You've already seen material extracted from *SOAN* essays, but I've barely scratched the surface. These essays vary from 2,000 to 10,000 words and are always readable and worthwhile. A few recent examples:

- "Discovery, rediscovery, and open access. Part 1." leads off issue #148 (August 2, 2010). At a little over 2,100 words, it's terse and addresses a "remarkable claim" by William Garvey: "in some disciplines, it is easier to repeat an experiment than it is to determine that the experiment has already been done."
- While most essays dissect serious situations or consider legislative issues, some are more lighthearted. So, for example, in April 2010 you'll find "A verb for the act [of] providing open access," a 2,000-word lark following up on Suber's contest for such a verb. Suber received 170 ideas from 51 people and describes both the ideas and why he's a "diction conservative" (including something I hadn't realized: Suber was reluctant to use *green OA* and *gold OA* because the terms aren't self-explanatory).
- "Four analogies to clean energy" is a longer (4,500 words) and more thought-provoking essay in the February 2010 issue. Read it; I almost guarantee it will make you think.

I could go on listing examples, but you get the idea. There's a wealth of good material here. The roundups are also great ways to find more information.

There's also a SPARC Open Access Forum (SOAF), a moderated discussion forum in list form. You'll find subscription links and a link to the forum archive at www.arl.org/sparc/publications/soan/. Look at the archive before subscribing to this list. List traffic isn't heavy—typically a few messages per day, some 5,500 over seven years.

OA tracking project. If I'd written this book a year ago, I would have identified *Open Access News* (OAN), by Peter Suber and, later, Gavin Baker, as the key way to track daily developments in open access, if in a somewhat overwhelming manner. OAN, a blog, typically had 5 to 25 posts each day. In its first years, it was comprehensive, becoming more selective as the volume of OA-related news increased. OAN still exists at www.earlham.edu/~peters/fos/fosblog.html, with more than 18,000 posts between May 2002 and April 2010—but it's no longer being updated. The archive is searchable.

Suber now recommends OATP, the OA tracking project, as the best way to keep up with daily events in open access. It's a social tagging project using Connotea (tag "oa.new" and a range of subtags). To learn more about OATP and find ways to follow the tags (via RSS or directly as a "blog-like web page"), visit http://oad.simmons.edu/oadwiki/OATP_FAQ. The bloglike page is www.connotea.org/tag/oa.new.

OATP is a work in progress but is certainly active. When I checked the bloglike page on February 5, 2010, there were 6,833 items. Checking again on September 27, 2010 (234 days later) I find 10,164, so the site's averaging around 14 new items per day. Take a look at OATP. Should you track it? Should you contribute to it by tagging OA-related items that others might miss?

The Access Principle. A book by John Willinsky, *The Access Principle: The Case for Open Access to Research and Scholarship* (Cambridge and London: The MIT Press, 2006, ISBN 978-0-262-51266-4). It's not entirely about open access (that's primarily the first 37 pages of a 287-page book) but it's well worth reading. Here's what Peter Suber had to say:

> John Willinsky understands the way the Internet changes everything for scholarly communication and has written a clear and compelling defense of open access, both in principle and in practice. I recommend it especially for its treatment of copyright issues and the special situation of scholarly societies and developing countries.[1]

The ISBN above is for the 2006 trade paperback; the clothbound edition appeared in 2005 for $37, while the trade paperback lists for $18 (and is available for $14.50 online—or $10 as an e-book).

Until Peter Suber's book appears in 2011, this is the best single-author philosophical treatment of open access issues. (My own collection, noted later in this chapter, is an unedited collection that is neither philosophical nor a coherent narrative text.)

I would have said that *The Access Principle* is not itself open access—and, as with the book you're reading now, that's reasonable, given that it's a monograph rather than a research paper. However, MIT also made the book available under a Creative Commons license, in 2006, at https://mitpress.mit.edu/books/willinsky/TheAccessPrinciple_The MITPress_0262232421.pdf. I'd suggest reading a few pages of the OA version of the book to decide whether the book works for you (Willinsky's style may not be for everybody), then buying the paperback if it does.

Willinsky uses open access to describe a broader range of items than most OA advocates. So, for example, journals that make articles freely available after a full year's embargo fall into one of Willinsky's ten varieties of open access. That may be a useful compromise to improve overall access. You'd need to read the book to understand more of Willinsky's thinking.

Transforming Scholarly Publishing through Open Access. Charles W. Bailey Jr. has been writing about and participating in open access since long before the term was coined, beginning with the founding of the *Public-Access Computer Systems Review* in 1989. He's published a variety of related bibliographies and webliographies over the years, most recently *Transforming Scholarly Publishing Through Open Access: A Bibliography*, ISBN 9781453780817, published in September 2010 by Digital Scholarship and available through Amazon.

Bailey contributed an earlier open access bibliography to the Open Access Directory (see below), where it has become the *Bibliography of open access*, lacking the prefatory material of the original but making it into a living work with contributions by other OAD contributors. That bibliography—which functions as a live set of links, but does not include annotation—continues to grow.

Bailey's Digital Scholarship page at http://digital-scholarship.org/ includes links to a range of other resources, including Bailey's blog (noted later) and the *Open Access*

Webliography (http://digital-scholarship.org/cwb/oaw.htm), an annotated set of links to a wide variety of web resources somehow related to open access.

Open Access Directory. *OAD* "is a compendium of simple factual lists about open access (OA) to science and scholarship, maintained by the OA community at large." It's a wiki, founded in April 2008 by Robin Peek of Simmons College and Peter Suber, at http://oad.simmons.edu/oadwiki. OAD does not contain argumentation. Instead, it provides facts, although some of those facts are lists of other places where you'll find lots of argumentation. As the "About" page says, "As far as possible, the OAD lists will be limited to brief factual statements without narrative or opinion."

One major virtue of OAD's limited scope is that it yields a resource you can make sense of. As of late September 2010, it includes some 220 content pages and shows just over a million page views.

This is another resource you can help improve and maintain as you become more familiar with open access. It's a great way to check up on some things—for example, disciplinary repositories or journals that have converted to OA (more than you might expect!)—and worth exploring.

BLOGS

The OAD "Blogs about OA" page lists nearly two hundred blogs, some of them blogs that occasionally mention OA topics, others blogs wholly concerned with OA. It's an interesting list if you want to explore deeply and particularly if you're multilingual. What I don't see on that page are blogs that oppose open access. One multipurpose blog, *the scholarly kitchen*, http://scholarlykitchen.sspnet.org/, has a higher concentration of anti-OA posts than any other I can think of.

Here are a few OA-related blogs you might find worthwhile. The blogs appear in alphabetical order.

Be Openly Accessible or Be Obscure. "A blog about topics related to the Open Access movement" by Jim Till at http://tillje.wordpress.com/. Till offers thoughtful commentary on a range of OA topics. As with most other surviving OA-related blogs, you won't be flooded with posts.

The Book of Trogool. "E-research, cyberinfrastructure, data curation, open access . . . an academic librarian examines how computers change research and libraries." This is Dorothea Salo's blog, at http://scientopia.org/blogs/bookoftrogool/. (The subtitle is from an earlier version.) The blog is now multi-authored, with contributions from Elizabeth Brown and Sarah Shreeves.

This blog covers a range of topics. Salo may be the field's most honest writer on real-world issues with institutional repositories, and takes a far more nuanced view of IRs than Stevan Harnad.

DigitalKoans. "What is the sound of one e-print downloading?" Charles W. Bailey Jr.'s blog on digital scholarship includes strong emphases on digital copyright, digital curation, digital and institutional repositories, and open access. You'll find it at http://digital-scholarship.org/digitalkoans/.

The Imaginary Journal of Poetic Economics. Here's the lengthy subtitle for this blog from Heather Morrison:

> Imagine a world where anyone can instantly access all of the world's scholarly knowledge—as profound a change as the invention of the printing press. Technically, this is within reach. All that is needed is a little imagination, to reconsider the economics of scholarly communications from a poetic viewpoint.

Morrison, a Canadian, is 100% in favor of open access, brooks no doubts on the matter, and writes both argumentative posts and sometimes slightly hyperbolic items such as her series of posts on "Dramatic Growth of Open Access."

OA Librarian. "Open Access resources by and for librarians" at http://oalibrarian.blogspot.com/. A group blog currently involving seven contributors, primarily very brief posts linking to other resources. Heather Morrison is one of the contributors to this blog.

Open Access Archivangelism. Stevan Harnad's blog, at http://openaccess.eprints.org/. Harnad is one of the founders of the open access movement and is the most forceful green OA advocate. His style will not suit everyone.

Open and Shut? This blog, by Richard Poynder, includes essays and interviews with various people, most of them associated with open access. Some blog posts provide introductions to interviews and link to full interviews, commonly in PDF form. You'll find it at http://poynder.blogspot.com/.

It's not all interviews. Direct essays can be lengthy and are always well written. For example, "Free our data: For democracy's sake" (June 28, 2010) runs nearly 3,600 words, longer than this chapter.

OptimalScholarship. "Alma Swan's weblog: An occasional commentary on issues that affect the progress of scholarship." You'll find it at http://optimalscholarship.blogspot.com/, but as of August 2010, there's a "possible violation of terms of service" flag in front of the blog. The most recent post—of a total of 19—is from July 23, 2009, and it's not clear that Swan plans to maintain this blog. That would be unfortunate, as the essays provide interesting personal perspectives on open access and data.

The Parachute. "It only works when it is open." Jan Velterop's blog offering essays on publishing and open access, is at http://theparachute.blogspot.com. The most recent post is November 10, 2009. It's fair to say that Velterop strongly favors gold OA over green OA.

BOOKS AND DIRECTORIES

Open Access: Key Strategic, Technical and Economic Aspects. This 2006 book from Chandos (edited by Neil Jacobs, ISBN 978-1843342038) is a collection of essays from a variety of people involved in OA. Preprints of most chapters are available in self-archived form, starting at www.eprints.org/community/blog/index.php?/archives/93 -Open-Access-Key-Strategic-Technical-and-Economic-Aspects.html.

Open Access and Libraries. This book is a collection of my OA-related essays in *Cites & Insights* from 2001 through 2009. It's a 513-page 6-by-9 trade paperback or the equivalent in PDF form. It's unedited and lacks an index, but includes all of the essays (and one bonus essay) in chronological order.

I can't recommend it as a coherent treatise on OA because it's not—and it's too long and piecemeal to recommend as a key source. You may find it useful as a supplemental resource. The text of the book is automatically licensed using the Creative Commons BY-NC license (since it comes from *Cites & Insights*), and the book page on Lulu, at http:// lulu.com/content/8764834 (or within http://stores.lulu.com/waltcrawford), includes a link for a free PDF download underneath the paperback purchase link (the paperback is priced at $17.50, $14.88 of which goes for production costs). Look for "Also available as File Download Free" below the "Add to Cart" button, and click on "File Download."

Directory of Open Access Journals. Maintained by Lund University Libraries, this directory "covers free, full text, quality controlled scientific and scholarly journals. We aim to cover all subjects and languages." In the colorful language of OA, *DOAJ* covers gold OA. Its web address is www.doaj.org.

As of September 27, 2010, the directory includes 5,437 journals, 2,276 of which can be searched at article level directly from *DOAJ*—including more than 446,000 articles.

If you're trying to make sense of *DOAJ* or get a sense of scope for this portion of open access, one good way to start is to expand the subject tree on the home page. That gives you a much longer two- and three-level subject list including a journal count for each subheading. So, for example, there are 113 open access journals under *Library and information science*, which is included in social sciences—and, to take an outstanding example, 163 OA mathematics journals (and another 37 statistics journals).

DOAJ isn't complete and includes journals that may not have proper peer review, but it's an outstanding place to start.

OTHERS

A few items that don't seem to fit elsewhere and that can also help keep you informed. I don't know of any journals other than *SPARC Open Access Newsletter* that are solely devoted to OA, but the first five items listed below are journals (not always refereed journals) that frequently include OA-related articles.

Ariadne Magazine. *Ariadne* is a quarterly e-journal from the UK, published by UKOLN and concerned with digital library initiatives and related technological developments.

Ariadne began in 1996. You'll find it at www.ariadne.ac.uk/. A search for "Open Access" yields 180 results, six of which have that phrase in their titles.

ARL: A Bimonthly Report and Research Library Issues: A Bimonthly Report . . . This bimonthly published 261 issues as *ARL: A Bimonthly Report on Research Library Issues and Actions from ARL, CNI, and SPARC* before changing to *Research Library Issues: A Bimonthly Report from ARL, CNI, and SPARC* in February 2009. The publication "reports on current issues of interest to academic and research library administrators, staff, and users." You'll find links to the current issue and archives of both publications at www .arl.org/resources/pubs/rli/index.shtml.

D-Lib Magazine. *D-Lib* has a "primary focus on digital library research and development" and currently appears six times a year. Produced by the Corporation for National Research Initiatives (CNRI), *D-Lib* began in July 1995; all issues are available online at www.dlib.org/dlib.html. A search for "open access" yields 1,172 matches, but that's a word search and includes stemming.

The Journal of Electronic Publishing. *JEP* "is a forum for research and discussion about contemporary publishing practices, and the impact of those practices upon users." Published by the Scholarly Publishing Office of the University of Michigan University Library, *JEP* began in 1995 and typically appears three times a year (with a three-year interruption from 2003 through 2005). Issues are at www .journalofelectronicpublishing.org.

Research Information. *Research Information* is a European bimonthly color print magazine. Its articles are freely available online from www.researchinformation.info, which also includes news items. The online archive dates back to May 2004 and, as of September 2010, includes at least 80 features on open access (recent issues appear not to be fully tagged).

ACRL Scholarly Communications Toolkit. This set of resources at http://scholcomm .acrl.ala.org "is an educational resource primarily directed to librarians."

> Its primary purpose is to assist librarians in (1) integrating a scholarly communication perspective into library operations and programs and (2) preparing presentations on scholarly communication issues for administrators, faculty, staff, students, or other librarians.

Reshaping Scholarly Communication. Another set of resources, this one from the Association of Research Libraries (ARL) at www.arl.org/sc/. As with the ACRL toolkit above, this site covers more than OA but includes some useful OA-related pages.

***SPARC Resources* on Open Access.** This subset of *SPARC Resources*, at www.arl.org/ sparc/openaccess/, provides some additional resources. You may also find the broader SPARC resources useful.

JISC Digital Repositories. JISC, a UK agency that "inspires UK colleges and universities in the innovative use of digital technologies," maintains a set of links to its many repository-related activities at www.jisc.ac.uk/whatwedo/topics/digitalrepositories.aspx.

Open Access Scholarly Information Sourcebook (OASIS). This site, at www.openoasis .org, has the subtitle "Practical steps for implementing Open Access"—it's decidedly an advocacy site. You'll find a handful of position papers (as of August 12, 2010, "What is open access?" and three papers related to institutional repositories), a few other "resources" tabs (at least one of them empty as of August 2010) and six "Users" tabs each leading to statements on why a particular group should support OA.

The STM report. This report was prepared for and published by IASTM, the International Association of Scientific, Technical and Medical Publishers. The 68-page document is available at www.stm-assoc.org/2009_10_13_MWC_STM_Report.pdf. The document provides the publisher perspective and denigrates the effectiveness and potential of OA at every turn. It's worth reading, but only while understanding the bias involved. If you're a librarian and understand budget issues, this paragraph from page 62 may give you a sense of how this report works:

> The value for money that the Big Deal and similar licences have brought, has largely contributed to the ending of the serials crisis, though that is not to say that the issue of journals cancellations has gone away.

Do you believe the serials crisis has ended? If so, you may find this report wholly convincing—and this Special Report largely useless. Otherwise, read, but read with care.

NOTE

1. MIT Press page for *The Access Principle*, http://mitpress.mit.edu/catalog/item/default .asp?tid=10611&ttype=2.

INDEX